May

P9-ECB-841

Dear Son, Bob:

Mortal life with its successes and failures, its joys and sorrows, its advancements and retreats is a trial and error and repentance prelude to eternity.

Many of life's entanglements will have to be unsnarled in the Millenium... for man is that he might have joy; and being unequally yoked is not productive of joy. You will find your companion and your joy prior to the Millenium, thanks to events that are painful and distressing now.

I see the Hand of the Lord in these events.... for your benefit. Love, Dad

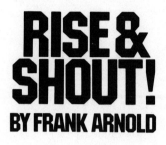

RISE & SHOUT!

BY FRANK ARNOLD

Generation Press, Inc., Orem, Utah.

Copyright © 1980 by Frank H. Arnold. *All rights reserved.* Published by Generation Press, Inc., Orem, Utah.

ISBN 0-936852-02-X

To my loving wife Bee and our five wonderful children, Kelly, Kristyn, Kippline, Gibson, and Kaline.

We wish to expressively thank the following for use of photos throughout the book:

Brigham Young University Sports Information
The Daily Herald
University of Oregon
Idaho State College
UCLA
Kurt Krieger

Generation Press°

TABLE OF CONTENTS

FOREWORD

Frank Arnold, a basketball coach, has written this autobiographical story in such an open, honest, sincere manner, typical of the man himself, that it is certain to be of interest to all readers regardless of whether or not they are interested in the sport of basketball.

He explains the origin of his initial interest in basketball and the trials and tribulations experienced along the way toward the successful attainment of his present position as head basketball coach at a major university. Although it was not an easy road for him, you will see that it remained a road of love that never permitted adversity to deter him from his objective. Furthermore, this goal was achieved without the sacrifice of ethical or moral principles.

As a matter of fact, one of the determining factors in my hiring him as an assistant at UCLA in 1971 was because of the fact that in addition to his professional qualifications he was reputed to be a fine family man of excellent moral character. Incidentally, this report proved to be accurate in his four years with us.

Coach Arnold's experiences as a player who had to study and work especially hard at the sport, as a high school teacher/coach, and as a college assistant coach at strikingly different colleges in vastly dissimilar locales under head coaches of contrasting styles of play and individual personality all helped him acquire a sound foundation for the achievement of his goal. These factors are discussed very openly as are some of the problems faced by coaches and others in the position of leadership during the rebellious sixties, the intricacies of recruiting, the value of faith, and the need for family, fan, and peer support.

It truly pleased me that Frank Arnold asked me to write the foreword to this story of his professional life to date. Like all of my ex-players and assistants, he is a part of my family.

John Wooden
UCLA-Retired

ACKNOWLEDGMENTS

My life has been touched by so many special people that it is difficult to acknowledge all of them. The many years of enjoyment my work has brought to me would not have been possible without the enormous amount of effort from men and women of the various support groups. The secretaries, the custodians, the ticket managers, equipment managers, team managers, statisticians, trainers, team doctors, sports information people and members of the media.

I owe a particular debt of gratitude to the administration who gave me the opportunity of being the head coach at Brigham Young University—President Dallin H. Oaks, Ben E. Lewis, Dr. Clayne Jensen, Stan Watts; and the finest Athletic Director in the business, Glen Tuckett.

My deepest appreciation is extended to my special friends and assistant coaches over the years—Dale Corn, Jed Gibson, Nick Nelson, Gail Seimen, Vern Kindsfather, Denny Houston, "Skeets" O'Connell, Gary Cunningham, John McMullen, Roger Reid, and Harry Anderson.

Words are not adequate to express my gratitude to the two men that have had the most profound influence on my life in basketball, Steve Belko and John Wooden.

Thank you to Dave Lisonbee for encouraging me to write this book, and to my secretary Kathy Kuettel for typing the manuscript.

Thank you to the many fans over the years, for their support and for their "suggestions."

Thank you to the parents, wives, and girlfriends of my former players for sharing them.

The biggest thanks of all is reserved for the numerous young men who have played for me these past twenty plus years—the Payette Pirates, the B.Y. High Wildcats, the Pocatello Indians, the Clark College Penguins, the Oregon Ducks, the UCLA Bruins, and the most special group of all, the Brigham Young University Cougars.

GETTING HOOKED ON BASKETBALL

October, 1946. Pocatello, Idaho. Roosevelt Elementary vs. Washington Elementary. It was the most important game of my life, because it was the first. This is where it all began: An away game at that.

I was a sixth grader at Roosevelt. Several of my buddies talked me into riding my bike across town with them to take on a bunch of guys from Washington who felt they could "whip" us in a game of basketball. I was game, even though I had never been on a court in my twelve years of existence.

I don't remember ever touching the ball. I realize now that my teammates were wise beyond their years, because they had me convinced that I was a "defensive specialist." I recall faceguarding Danny Jones for the duration of the game—nose-to-nose, I believe we called it. When he caught the ball, I would invariably thump him in the forehead with the palm of my hand. He complained the whole game, but I just accused him of being a cry baby. Nobody had told me yet about "fouls."

I'm not sure who won, but our team must have, because I was hooked. I wanted more of this new game called basketball. I even wanted to try my hand at bouncing the ball and throwing it at the basket.

My father and mother, Gervase and Maxine Arnold, managed the old Rainbow Motel in Pocatello. There was a big laundry room for the tenants with a cement floor and very high ceiling. I talked my dad into buying me a rim and nailing it to the wall at one end of this triangular-shaped room. The only obstacle I had to worry about was the big shelf directly under the basket on which the ladies sorted their clothing. At any rate, it was my very own private gymnasium, and I spent many hours in there working on my dribbling and shooting.

The next fall I entered the 7th grade at Franklin Jr. High School, where my homeroom teacher also happened to be the basketball coach, Mr. Ivan Ball. Mr. Ball was from the state of Kentucky, and in

My father and mother Gervase and Maxine Arnold.

*In front of my laundry room gymnasium
with my older brothers Gene and Earl.*

that particular era the University of Kentucky was the hottest thing
going in baketball.

Mr. Ball allowed me to try out for the school team; and as good
fortune would have it, I was selected as one of the players. I can still
visualize our navy blue, wool uniforms with the small white flannel
numbers. Boy, was I proud! It was during this winter of 1947 that I
made one of the three most important decisions of my life: I was going
to be a basketball coach.

During the eighth grade a new fad hit our campus—G.I. crew
cuts. I don't recall how it started, but we team members couldn't wait
to get to the barber so that we could have our hair clipped as short as
possible without being bald.

The girls in school were really upset with this strange new look. In
protest a few of them had their hair cut in crew fashion back to the
crown of their head. Their protest was to no avail, however, as the new
look was sported by nearly all basketball players for the next dozen
years or so.

We only had two other junior high schools in the area, Irving and
Fort Hall. Our season, therefore, was limited to a grand total of four
games per year.

At Fort Hall we played in an old sunken swimming pool. The
deep end had been leveled off with concrete. The backboards were
hung on the pool walls at each end. If we touched any of the four walls,

it was considered out of bounds. We actually had to climb down a ladder in order to play the game.

Coach Ivan Ball and the Franklin Jr. High 7th grade team.

It was at Fort Hall where I had one of my moments of glory. I was never good enough to be a starter, but I was a heck of a sub. Coach Ball once inserted me into the game during a time-out. When the ball was put into play, both teams became confused and lined up at the opposite basket. My teammate passed the ball inbounds to me so that we could advance it up court. Instead, I promptly shot it at the basket I was standing under, and made two points. Everybody hollered at me for doing such a dumb thing and shooting at the wrong basket, but I somehow knew that it was the right basket. My teammate took it out of bounds amid the laughter and passed it to me again. I shot it again and made two more.

In exasperation, Mr. Ball called time out to get me straightened out. The referee, however, came to my defense and informed everyone that I was right, and they were wrong. To my delight, they counted my four points: my season high.

During the eighth grade my parents moved to North 11th Street, so my old laundry room gymnasium was no more. Instead, my closest friend, Bob Conley, and I leveled off a little area in my back yard. My dad hung the backboard on an A-frame swing he had made for us, and the CONOLD Arena was christened. Bob and I had many a great one-on-one contest on that hard dirt patch. The University of Utah had just completed a highly successful season, and since my nickname was Arnie, it was natural that I was Arnie Ferrin, and Bob was Vern Gardner or someone else during our numerous contests. Little did I realize that my hero in those days some thirty years later would be the Athletic Director of the school with which I would be pitted in our biggest rivalry each year.

When the snow fell and the CONOLD Arena became too muddy to play on, Bob and I would take our gloves and shovels and head for the asphalt courts at Franklin Junior High. Inevitably we would end up shoveling snow off one of the courts with two friends of ours, Paul Tueller and Arley Lish. I would be a rich man if I had a dollar for all the two-on-two contests we played until it was too dark to continue.

Putting one up at the CONOLD Arena (left), posing with my best friend Bob Conley.

As we grew older we would scour the city to find any gymnasium we could that was open for play. On a couple of occasions we even found some that were not open.

Word spread that the old Reed Gymnasium on the Idaho State College campus (it has since been torn down) was "break-inable," if you knew the right way. One Saturday afternoon during the summer, a few of the boys and I decided to give it a try. We climbed a tree adjacent to the building that enabled us to get on the roof by the side of the sky-lights. Once there, we could force a certain one open, climb into the gym, and work our way down some gymnastics wall ladders to the playing floor. A piece of cake!

We were having ourselves quite a ball in the solitude of this big-time court, when suddenly the front doors were flung open, and there stood an ISC football coach, Dutch Scheramin. We were scared to death. Dutch had heard the commotion as he passed by, and he decided to investigate. Fortunately for us he was quite understanding, and after a good lecture on breaking and entering he let us go. That was the last assault on Reed Gym.

Dick Burns, Paul Tueller and Bob.

The second assault on a closed gym was made about two and a half years later during the dead of winter. It was a cold Sunday afternoon. Bob and I and another close friend, Glenn Evans, decided to find a place to shoot after Sunday School. The only place we could find a back door open was the Pocatello LDS Second Ward Gymnasium.

Unlike most LDS church houses today, the gym was a separate wing connected to the main building. Once inside we found the gym to be nearly as cold as it was outside. After about 15 minutes, Glenn decided to do something about the cold. He knew where the furnace room was, and he went there to check things out. After some careful deductions, he turned a few valves and returned to the floor. Sure enough, within 15 to 20 minutes we could feel the warmth surround us. We had been practicing nearly one hour when a very irate man entered the gym from the hallway that led to the main building and chapel. His anger was not solely directed to the fact that we were playing basketball in the church gymnasium on Sunday. That was bad enough. But it seems as if Glenn had not only turned valves that allowed heat into the gym, he had also turned some that stopped the flow of heat into the chapel. Unknown to us, a sacrament service was being held at the same time, and the congregation had become increasingly less comfortable as it grew colder and colder.

In the fall of 1948, I entered Pocatello High School as a ninth grader. Our four-grade enrollment was about 2,100. There must have been over 200 boys try out for the frosh-soph basketball team. I was among the early casualties to be cut from the team. I was disappointed, but undaunted. Fortunately, our church had an outstanding basketball program for its youth, so I played that winter for the LDS 4th Ward junior M-Men team.

The following year I tried out for the frosh-soph club once again, but I ran into the same result. I was too short, too slow, and too weak; but I had a good attitude. Back to junior M-Men ball for another winter.

During the summer I grew several inches. Going into my junior year in high school I was 6'1" tall, and weighed a mighty 135 pounds. My zest for the game was even greater, so I reported for the junior varsity tryouts. The third time was the charm, for I was selected for the fifteen player squad. I had never been prouder in my entire life. My good friend Bob, however, was cut.

Our neighborhood team pitcher Dick Parrish and me.

Bob and I at graduation from Polly H.S.

About two weeks later on a Saturday morning, we were scheduled to have a special practice. It was still a week before our first game. I talked Bob into going to practice with me. When we arrived at the gym, our coach asked Bob if he would mind dressing down and practicing with us. It seemed that one of our players was sick and couldn't make it. Bob was obviously delighted, and worked his fool head off that morning. I was very pleased for him, but little did I realize the consequences of his fine performance.

On Monday as I reported for practice, the coach called me into his office. "Frank, I regret having to do this, but I am going to let you go." Would you believe that my very best friend had been given my spot on the team? At the tender age of sixteen, I found that moment to be one of the toughest things I had ever had to deal with.

I have long since learned two great lessons from that experience. First, one of the most difficult tasks in coaching is the necessity of cutting a young man from a squad. I didn't have much compassion for my coach on that particular day, but I have on many occasions since then had to go through the same unpleasant experience. After twenty years it doesn't get any easier. The heartache and trauma it causes for these young men is a hard thing for them to cope with—coaches share with them a part of that heartache.

That, in itself, is the second lesson I have learned. There are few, if any, mediums that offer young men and women as many opportunities to grow physically, mentally, socially, and emotionally, as does the world of athletics.

My senior year I went to bat for the fourth time and struck out again. This time the fifteenth spot was between me and a junior of equal ability. The coach kept the junior, explaining that he had two full years to develop, whereas I had only one. That didn't make sense to me at the time. I felt that since I was a senior and therefore my last chance, that the coach should have kept me. Now that I am a coach, it is considerably easier for me to understand. As cruel as it may seem at times, the needs of the team are of far greater importance than those of any one individual.

Well, whether I wanted to admit it or not, I simply was not a very good basketball player. Nevertheless, my ambition to become a basketball coach has never wavered from that winter day in the seventh grade. I was more determined than ever to be successful. I was hooked—and I was going to be a coach!

2

THE YEARS OF PREPARATION

I have often felt that three of the most important decisions a person makes during his lifetime are: (1) the person one chooses to marry, (2) the career one chooses to pursue, and (3) the college or university one chooses to attend in pursuit of that career.

Upon graduation from high school I was a long way from any decision pertaining to marriage. I was more fortunate than many, however, for I had long since decided what I wanted to be—a coach. The third decision now stared me in the face. Where should I go to college?

For years I had wanted to attend Brigham Young University. In reality, however, I simply did not have enough money saved, nor were my parents in a financial position to support me at BYU. However, we lived in Pocatello where Idaho State College was located. A semester's tuition for an in-state student was only $46.25. During the summer following high school I had worked as a highway survey crew man for $1.25 an hour and had been able to save enough for two semester's tuition plus a few bucks. I could still live at home, so room and board would not be an additional expense.

In the fall of 1956, I enrolled at Idaho State College with a dual major in Education—Physical Education, and a minor in mathematics. The first step was taken in pursuit of my chosen career.

That October I took the second step: I tried out for the ISC junior varsity basketball team. It was here where I first met a man who was to be very influential in my life, Steve Belko, the head baketball coach for the ISC Bengals. At this point he didn't know my name, for I was not even a high school letterman, let alone a grant-in-aid recipient. I had a goal, however, and I was determined to see it through.

I lasted two weeks before I was cut. I was extremely disappointed, but it was easy for me to see that I simply was not as talented nor experienced as the ten players they kept on the JV squad. Back to M-Men ball—disappointed, but not discouraged.

The Pocatello 4th Ward M-Men team with Al Hobson as coach.

It's difficult to evaluate just how much this LDS church league basketball program affected my life. I know that without it I would not be where I am today. Our Pocatello 4th Ward M-Men team was made up of all my playground buddies, Bob Conley, Glenn Evans, Paul Tueller, Arley Lish and several older players. Our coaches and advisors were two men who not only helped me with basketball in their limited capacity, but more importantly with life in general, Al Hobson and John R. "Doc" Davis.

Although I was a very ordinary basketball player, I played a fairly decent game of baseball. I had lettered my final two years at Poky High and was quite proud of my accomplishments. Unfortunately, ISC did not have a baseball team. I felt, however, that it was necessary for me to do something in the spring that might help me physically for the following winter since I intended to try out for the basektball team again. My buddy Bob was an exceptional track man, specializing in the 100 and 220 yard dashes. The decision was made. I would try out with Bob for the track team.

I wasn't fast, and I couldn't jump; so I chose an event in which I felt neither was important—the 880. Our track coach, Milton "Dubby" Holt was either a very patient man or exhibited a great deal of tolerance. In my case, it was a good measure of both. I believe that to this very day I still hold an ISC track and field record, for I was the only participant in ISC history to run in every track meet for the entire year and not be awarded one single point for placement.

I recall running three miles during each Monday practice. On every lap I would think to myself, "What a stupid sport—running around in circles to see who could get nowhere the fastest!" It was during the Monday laps that I formulated another game plan: To encourage ISC officials to adopt baseball as a spring sport.

About half way through the season, "Dubby" Holt came to me with a suggestion. "Frank, I want you to do something for me. I want you to run at exactly the same pace that you run the 880, but we will change your event to the two-mile." I suspect he thought a 2:12, 880 was not particularly awesome. Even at that same pace, I wouldn't have impressed anyone with my two-mile times.

The change was made, and I became a distance runner. People tend to forget unfavorable experiences, and quite honestly I cannot recall a single race I was in—except one—the Old Rocky Mountain Conference track meet held at Colorado College in Colorado Springs.

It was a cold, wet day. We had three runners entered in the two mile. Coach Holt had drawn the 3rd, 7th, and 33rd lanes. He gave me the 33rd. (I believe there were 36 entrants.) This was to be my last race. I was determined to do well. I decided that when the gun sounded I would sprint for all I was worth for the first 100 yards and get well up in the pack. When I looked up I was in last place. Mud splattered me from head to foot from the runners ahead of me. I guess everyone had the same idea.

As the race progressed, I surprised even myself as I slowly passed runner after runner. As I completed my sixth lap I glanced over my shoulder and could see the leading runner about 100 yards behind me nearing the completion of his seventh lap. I knew that he would begin his "kick" on his eighth and final lap and very possibly "lap" me. Well, I wasn't a very good runner either, but I was a competitor with a fair share of pride. As the gun sounded for his final lap, he started his kick. I, too, picked up my pace—he was not about to lap me. He was, however, gaining ground. With 220 to go, I led him by 25 yards. With

100 to go, my lead had been cut to 10 yards. To this day, I think the crowd actually thought I was in the lead. They were on their feet cheering like crazy. I started in a full sprint, but so did the guy chasing me. The officials did not even have time to get the tape up for him, for I nosed him at the final line by less than a yard. The crowd went nuts. I felt great—until I realized that I still had one lap to go. I finished in sixth place, but only five places received points. I had kept my record intact!

When basketball season rolled around my sophomore year, I was once again at the coach's doorstep requesting an opportunity to try out. (This was to be the sixth consecutive year that I would make an attempt to be selected for my school's basketball team.) My persistence finally paid off. I was selected to play for the ISC JV squad! My limited success was certainly reward enough for my many years of dedication and hard work. As the season progressed I played all three positions: center, forward, and guard.

Early in December our varsity team was scheduled to play BYU at Provo, but the JV team was not involved in the preliminary. Paul Tueller and I decided to drive down to see the game. A major snowstorm that very weekend made travel quite precarious. Nevertheless, we struck out for Provo at 12:00 noon in my 1942 Chevy. It had no heater, no defroster, no windshield wipers. We had the trunk filled with buckets of sand and a shovel. We had sweaters, coats, and blankets to keep us warm, since a good portion of the trip was made with my head out the window so that I could see where we were going. We also had to stop every 25 miles to add a quart of oil. The trip of 225 miles would normally take about four or five hours.

Paul and I parked the car at the Smith Fieldhouse parking lot, sprinted to the front lobby ticket windows, and entered the fieldhouse just as the referee tossed the ball up to start the game. It was 8:05 p.m. We were exhausted and nearly frozen, but we were where we wanted to be.

It was the first trip I had ever made to Provo, and the first time I had seen a BYU home game. The Cougars won, 63-50. I remember how impressed I was with student and community support. Little did I know at the time that someday I would have the privilege of being the head coach at this great institution.

As we were leaving the game, darned if we didn't see our old buddy from Poky, Glenn Evans! Glenn had driven his girl friend, LaRue Pugmire, to Provo that same afternoon in his new 1953 Oldsmobile. LaRue's sister was a BYU student. You can imagine our thoughts as we realized we could have made the trip in quick comfort with Glen, had we known he too was driving to Provo.

LaRue spent the night with her sister. After draining the water from my car's radiator so it wouldn't freeze, Glenn, Paul and I spent the night at a friend's home on a fold-out couch with one old army blanket to keep the three of us warm. Somehow we made it through the night.

The next day we visited several friends from Pocatello who were attending BYU. That night we saw the Cougars beat ISC again, 70-59. After another miserable night, we got my car running and headed home for Pocatello. Provo and BYU had left quite an impression on me.

During my junior year, Belko combined the JV and varsity squad so that everyone practiced together. There were twenty of us remaining after the initial cuts. At our first few home games I played in the JV games and then dressed down for the varsity games as well. Just before Christmas, Belko cornered me one day after practice and said, "Pack your bags, you've made the traveling squad, and we're leaving Christmas day for Buffalo, New York." You've never met a prouder young man in your life! I was finally a legitimate member of the varsity team.

1955-56 Idaho State College Bengals.

On Christmas morning, 1954, we met at the Union Pacific Train Depot in Pocatello to board the Portland Rose streamliner for what was to be a two-day trip to Buffalo. We were scheduled to play in the Canisus College Queen City Tournament in Buffalo from December 28 to January 2. It was my first big trip, and I was excited. My clothes were packed in the new suitcase Mom and Dad had given me for Christmas, and I was wearing a gray sportscoat over my favorite sportshirt. I was crushed when Belko chewed me out for not having a dress shirt and tie on for the journey. My first trip—I hadn't even gotten on the train yet, and I was in trouble.

The all-day, all-night ride on the Portland Rose was really quite enjoyable. Belko and a good number of the players were playing "hearts" most of the way. As I watched and studied the card game carefully, I slowly learned how it was played. It wasn't long before I could see that one of our "stars" was cheating his teammates more often than not.

In Chicago the next morning we changed from the Union Pacific Railroad to an eastern line. What a tremendous difference there was in comfort and service! From Chicago to Buffalo we were treated more like cattle going to a slaughterhouse than like paying customers. We arrived in Buffalo about 8:00 p.m. December 26. We arrived in Buffalo about 8:00 p.m. December 26. Our reception committee met us and took us to the Peter Stuyvesant Hotel. My roommate was Norman "Duke" Wiseman, a fellow I grew very fond of during my four years at ISC.

The next day after our practice session we were guests at a private banquet on the campus of Canisus College. Our host was a Catholic Priest who was apparently an administrator at Canisus. I was seated next to the priest, who in turn was seated next to Coach Belko. As the waitress began to serve us, I turned my coffee cup over to show that I did not want to be served coffee. Gerry Hicks, one of our team members, did likewise. What happened next has been a life-long testimony to me of the importance of living one's standards, particularly religious ones, with firm conviction. The Catholic priest turned to Coach Belko and proclaimed, "Apparently those two young men don't care much for our Irish coffee." Coach Belko replied, "No, that's not the reason. Those two boys are Mormons, and Mormons don't drink coffee." Belko then proceded to give the priest a brief explanation of the LDS Word of Wisdom. I was astonished for two reasons. First, I didn't realize that my coach even knew that I was a Mormon, or had any knowledge of the Word of Wisdom. Second, the simple act of turning my cup over led to a discussion of my religion and a way of life which I have always been very proud of. Since that very day I have tried to be particularly careful to uphold my religious convictions, regardless of the environment in which I found myself.

The next day was game day. As was our custom, we met for our pre-game meal four hours prior to game time. Coach Belko would see that we were all together and then leave us to our privacy while he took a short walk. The same player that I suspected of cheating at cards on the train promptly talked one of the waitresses into bringing him a couple of "Old Fashions" for two silver dollars. Silver dollars were practically unheard of at that time in New York, and she was quick to agree to the arrangement. Being a naive kid from Pocatello, I assumed an "Old Fashion" was a side dish or sandwich or something. I was deeply shocked when the waitress brought him two shots of an alcoholic beverage. The pre-game meal, no less. For his trick, that player lost the respect of a great number of his teammates, including mine.

As we were dressing for the game, the same player informed Belko that he had forgotten the belt to his game uniform. Belko made me give him mine. That was really a put-down. Giving this "character" my belt no doubt meant that I would not see any game action. My exhilaration of making the varsity squad was quickly tempered by the reality of just how valuable I really was to the team.

Our first game was against Georgia Tech. We had two outstanding forwards, Les Ron and Lloyd Harris. Les was only 6 feet 1 inch, and Lloyd was about 6 feet 3 inches. They were small by major college standards today, but both were exceptional outside shooters. On alternate trips down the court they seemed to take turns making 18-20 foot one-handed jump shots and set shots. One-handed set shots were not as common as the two-handed variety in the east during the 50's, and the crowd was really buzzing while Les and Lloyd put on quite a show.

At one time during the game we were lined up along the free throw lane for a two-shot foul attempt. When the first shot was made, a Georgia Tech player recovered the ball from the net and tossed it toward the referee administering the free throw. The Tech player threw the ball so low, however, that the ref couldn't handle it. He had to chase the ball as it rolled to the other end of the floor. The Tech player turned to Les, and with a big grin on his face said in his southern drawl, "That's my fav-o-rite trick."

We eventually lost the game 69-72. The next day we had a bye, so Coach Belko gave us the evening off with instructions to be back in the hotel no later than midnight. Duke and I caught a cab and went downtown to see the sights. We took in a late movie, and by the time we got back to the hotel it was nearly 12:30. When we got out of the cab we could see Belko sitting in the lobby. I was scared to death. There was no way that I was going to be caught breaking curfew on my very first road trip. We sneaked around to the back of the hotel and searched until we found a service entrance door still open. We worked our way through a maintenance area and up the back stairs until we were safe inside our room.

The next day we played Yale and beat them 70-69. They had a player named Chet Forte who is now a heavyweight with CBS television sports programming.

The following night we were to play Fordham for the consolation championship. Belko called for a 4 p.m. meeting in his room. Duke and I screwed up again and got to the meeting about five minutes late. We both got a pretty good tongue-lashing from Belko. He threatened to give us both a one-way bus ticket back home. I was thoroughly convinced that he meant it. Later when we met outside the hotel to catch the taxi cabs to the game, Belko insisted that Duke and I ride with him so that we wouldn't get lost on the way to the game. Boy, did I feel great. No tie...late for curfew...late for our only meeting...being babysat by the coach. I was off to a great start. Fordham, with the great All-American Ed Conlin, beat us 72-63.

From that Queen City Tournament on, it was all uphill as we won the Rocky Mountain Conference Championship for the third consecutive year. We were consequently scheduled to play Seattle University in the NCAA Western Regional Tournament at the Cow Palace in San Francisco. The other two teams involved were the University of San Francisco and West Texas State.

The Cow Palace was semi-appropriately named. It was certainly not a palace, but it was indeed a place for cows. I believe I would have named it, "The Big Yellow Barn for Cows." A basketball pavilion it was not.

We dressed in a small upstairs room with no lockers or hangers. We simply folded our clothes and laid them on the floor. After our half-time meeting, USF moved in and used the same dressing room. From this room we walked at least 100 yards past a row of cattle corrals, ankle deep in dirt and cow manure, to the portable playing floor. The arena seated 13,000, and at the time it seemed bigger than the entire population of Pocatello.

We lost to a fine Seattle University team, 80-63. As we trudged back to the dressing room I passed a big lanky USF player with one of his exceptionally long arms draped around his coach (Phil Woolpert), offering him some advice as they walked down the staircase from the dressing room. He was the now legendary Bill Russell.

I dressed hurriedly, as I was anxious to see Russell, K.C. Jones, and the rest of the number one team in America play. They were undefeated at the time, and of course went on to win the NCAA championship. During the game I saw USF execute a play that absolutely awed me. I am convinced that this play was responsible for a major revision of the rules the next year.

Up to and including the 1954-55 season, the keyhole in high school and college baketball was shaped like the keyholes in the doors of older homes. That is, the free throw lane was only six feet across from the baseline to the jump circle which was, of course, twelve feet in diameter. Russell would plant himself in the low post on the left side with his back to the basket. Because the key was so narrow he was only three feet from the hoop. K.C. Jones would bring the ball down to the wing on the same side and then lob a pass to Russell. Bill would jump into the air, catch the ball with one hand as easily as most people would catch a softball, spin and slam dunk the ball all in one motion. With his long arms, big hands, and incredible jumping ability, it was virtually an impossible shot to stop. The rule makers could easily see that the big man could destroy the game if he was allowed to station himself that close to the hoop. That spring they legislated against such a probability when they voted to widen the keyhole to twelve feet, the same as it is today.

I have a vivid recollection of the adjustment we had to make in our offensive and defensive strategies as we grew accustomed to the new keyhole my senior year. It amazed me that the wider lane affected the game as much as it did. Overnight there seemed to be more scoring opportunities for the guards and forwards who were skilled drivers. The constantly congested middle had been opened up. On the other hand, the big man was not as dominant as he once was.

I was becoming more confident in my game. It appeared as if Belko was too, in that he alternated me between the fifth and sixth man during our pre-season practice sessions. He even saw to it that my scholarship job was improved from shining the brass in the swimming pool to refereeing intramural water polo games. That was a super job, because there were no teams. All I had to do three nights a week was show up at the swimming pool at game time, wait fifteen minutes until a forfeit was declared, draw my pay, and go home.

Our first game of the year was a home game against Utah State. I did not start, but I was quite certain I would be the first sub off the bench. USU had a great guard from Chicago named Pat Dunn. As the game progressed, Dunn was giving us fits. It was obvious that we were going to have to stop him if we expected to win. Belko called for me to get ready. He gave me firm instructions on how to defend him. "Gotcha, Coach," I replied and reported into the game—my big chance to make good.

The first time down the court Dunn started to drive straight toward me. I stood my ground and forced him to dribble to his right into the deep corner. I thought I had him. Without breaking stride he went into the air with a running right-handed hook shot from at least twenty feet. Swish—two points. I couldn't believe it. Nobody shoots a running hook shot from twenty feet!

The next time down he started at me again. No way was I going to let him go right this time. I quickly over-played him and forced him to the left. Would you believe he did the same thing, only this time with a left-handed hook. Swish—two points. I didn't dare look at Belko.

Third time down he started straight at me once more. I think he thought he had a pigeon. I honestly didn't know what to do this time. He veered to the right, and I went with him; he crossed over and cut back going left—I stayed with him until WHACK! I ran straight into a screen set by the USU center and ended up in a heap at his feet. Dunn threw up his third consecutive running hook. Same tune: Swish—two points.

Belko called a quick time-out—got the hook out and had me on the bench before the band could strike up its first note. That was the last game that I was the sixth man . . . or seventh . . . or eighth. As a matter of fact, when our SID published our team statistics, he only itemized the first ten players. The rest of the players' stats were lumped together under the heading "others." I was one of the "others."

I nearly made an early entrance into the University of Utah game two weeks later, however. The game was in Salt Lake City. I believe the Utes were ranked about second in the nation at the time. At any rate, they had a great team: Bergan, Bundy, Buckwalter, etc.

Utah jumped to an early lead. Not too far into the game Belko called out "ARNOLD!" I quickly took off my warmup pants and hurried up the bench to sit next to him. I sat there waiting for him to give me instructions who to sub for. About thirty seconds later he said,

"DETHLEFS." Bryce Dehtlefs quickly took off his warm-up and slid in between Belko and me. It wasn't but another thirty seconds when Belko called out "WISEMAN." Bryce and I both slid down to make room for Duke. About three minutes and four players later, I was back down at the end of the bench where I started.

Coach Belko was not what I would classify as a referee baiter. As with all coaches, he had his moments of anguish. One of our favorite stories about him was supposed to have taken place at Bozeman, Montana, in a game against Montana State. I'm really not sure if the incident is true or not, but it sure is a good story.

It seems as if the Bengals were getting a pretty good "homer" job this particular evening. A fifth foul call on one of our starters was the final straw. Belko met the official face to face as he approached the scorer's bench. Taking his wallet out of his hind pocket, Belko threw it at the referee's feet and shouted, "Here, take this, you robber, you've got everything else."

For the fourth consecutive year, Coach Belko's ISC team won the Rocky Mountain Conference Championship and was admitted to the first round of the NCAA tournament. This time we were to play at the University of Washington's Hec Edmundson Pavilion in Seattle. Our opponent was once again to be our old nemesis Seattle University. Our best player, Les Roh, was ruled ineligible for the tournament because he had played varsity ball as a freshman. Nevertheless, his replacement Gail Seiman played exceptionally well, and our team played a great game, only to lose a heartbreaker 68-66.

It was all over. My collegiate playing days had ended. As I sat in the Vistadome of the Portland Rose streamliner on our way back to Pocatello, I contemplated my future. The moon was full. I sat alone as we rode down the Columbia River Gorge. The beauty and serenity of the evening will forever linger in my memory. Late into the night I pondered the same questions over and over. "Where would I be a year from today?" "How will I go about getting a job?" "Will I, in fact, be hired some place as a coach?"

There was to be one more basketball trip before I had to seek the answer to these questions, however. We arrived back in Pocatello late Sunday night. Monday afternoon at school I was approached by some of my friends. They had entered a team in an outlaw tournament in Elko, Nevada. They invited me to go along as one of eight players. We had to leave Tuesday, for the first game was to be played Wednesday night.

I explained that I was nearly broke, and I wasn't sure if I could afford to go. "No problem," they insisted. The rooms only cost $12 per night, and we would share the cost with four guys to a room. That would amount to only $3 a night for three nights, or $9. Food should be no more than $10 for the three days. Besides that, prize money would be awarded for the first three places, and we were sure to win something. I had $20, so I figured, what the heck. It sounded like fun, and I could probably squeeze by on my $20.

We left the next day after classes and arrived in Elko about 8 p.m. After checking into our hotel rooms we went directly to the casino. It was my first trip to Nevada, and the slot machines and gambling tables fascinated me. My good friend, Bob Hodge, and I walked around for a good hour watching people gambling. We both became particularly intrigued with the "21" table. That game was easy. The temptation was too great. I was about to learn a great lesson in life. Over the long haul, gamblers never really win. As soon as a couple of chairs were vacated, we jumped at the opportunity to enter the game. I bought $10 worth of chips. The game was played for a minimum of $1 per hand. For the first thirty minutes or so I was about even. Then I started to win a few extra bucks. As is usually the case, however, my lucky streak ended, and within an hour or so I had lost my $10. But then I thought, "I'll go for ten more, and as soon as I build it back up to $20 I'll quit." After all, I had been a winner up until just a couple of successive bad hands. I could easily do it again.

I shelled out my last $10. This time, however, it went pure and fast. Within minutes I was flat broke. Three days to go, and I had but one copper penny in my pocket. That was hardly enough to eat on for the next three days.

Bob proved to be a better blackjack player than me. It took him nearly three hours before he lost all of his money. What a couple of big-time operators we were! Exactly one penny between the two of us. It was near midnight, so we trudged up to bed. Maybe the dawn of a new day would enlighten our predicament.

We awoke about 9 a.m. Our other two roomies had already left for breakfast. No such luck for Bob and me. After dressing we started downstairs. Maybe we could talk some of our buddies into a small loan. We had to walk past a row of slot machines on our way to the coffee shop. As luck would have it, I spotted a nickel on the floor under one of the slots. I picked it up and told Bob, "Watch this, I'm going to hit a jackpot." I inserted the nickel and pulled the crank. Well, I didn't hit a jackpot, but darned if four nickels didn't come tumbling into the tray!

"That's it!" I exclaimed. "I've got the answer." "What in the devil are you talking about?" Bob asked. "Look," I said. "A penny and these four nickels make a total of 21¢. There's a small grocery store next door, and we can buy one of those small loafs of bread for 21¢." We headed out the door, not saying another word to each other, but both realizing what else we would have when we departed from the grocery store. Sure enough, the store carried the 21¢ loaves. We bought one and left. When we got back to our room, we also had a 24-slice pack of American cheese. The manner in which we acquired the cheese taught me that one foolish wrong doing, gambling, leads to another foolish wong doing, stealing.

For the next three days our breakfasts, lunches, and dinners each consisted of one cheese sandwich apiece. Occasionally we would go to the coffee shop and talk the waitresses into free patties of butter, cups of hot water, and ketchup. I had often heard my friends talk about a cheap way to make tomato soup, but I didn't think I would ever try it. It was kind of weak, but with plenty of salt it wasn't bad.

We won the first game, lost the second, and won the third. That gave us third place and a total of $80 prize money. Of course we split it eight ways, and my $10 share enabled me to pay my $9 hotel bill. I generously donated my last dollar to our driver for gas. I returned to Pocatello weaker, but wiser.

Well, my four year college stint was rapidly coming to a close. I had successfully completed one of my goals, would surely complete a second, but I was still in a quandary as to the third.

First. I had made the varsity basketball team and had earned two letters. Although I didn't letter in track, I did earn two more letters in baseball: it had been initiated as a varsity sport my junior year.

Second. I had done quite well academically and would graduate with a 3.13 accumulative GPA with a BS degree in Education-Physical Education and a mathematics minor.

Third. This goal was still ahead of me—to secure a head coaching job. My academic counselor, Dr. Byrne Fernelius, kept exhorting me to relax and not worry about it. "We'll get you a job," he kept saying. "Quit worrying about it." I did worry about it, however. I had been working towards that goal for ten long years and did not want to be denied.

3

MY FIRST
COACHING JOB

Dr. Fernelius was true to his word. By the first of May he had lined up two job interviews for me. One was for head basektball coach at Hailey, Idaho, a small town about twenty miles south of Sun Valley. Skiing was, of course, the big winter sport there, and the basketball program had long been suffering. In a telephone conversation with the superintendent we set the interview for the following Friday afternoon at the high school.

The second possibility was for the head basketball and head baseball job at Payette High School, also in Idaho. Payette is located in the Snake River Valley, about sixty miles east of Boise near the Idaho-Oregon border. This particular job intrigued me much more than the one at Hailey. I phoned the superintendent, and we arranged the interview for Thursday morning. This would give me ample time to drive to Hailey for the Friday appointment.

Wednesday afternoon I drove to Boise and spent the night with some friends. Early Thursday morning I set out for Payette. As I approached the town, down the long gradual decline of the highway, I was impressed with the setting of this tree-laden community in the valley, with the Snake River passing by. A sense of unexplained excitement came over me. Perhaps this would be where my professional career would begin.

I met with the Superintendent of Schools, Mr. Donovan L. Douglas, in his office at the high school. He introduced me to the principal, Mr. Leo Palumbo. I was particularly impressed with Mr. Palumbo, a bright gregarious guy with curly hair, mustache and big smile. He took me around the school introducing me to a variety of people and then on a tour of the athletic facilities. It was here that I had my first negative impression. The gymnasium was an old, poorly lighted building adjacent to the classroom area. The floor was dark brown in color, having not been refinished in its thirty years of existence. The bleachers were permanent, solid wood benches. The most distressing factor was that there were only two baskets, one on each end of the floor, and no room for additional auxiliary practice baskets.

The baseball diamond was skinned out of one corner of the football field. The left field fence was, therefore, 350 feet from home plate, and the right field fence only 225 feet. The bleachers and dugouts were in a terrible state of disrepair.

After the tour of the school and the meeting of some influential townspeople, we went back to the superintendent's office. Mr. Douglas and Mr. Palumbo asked me what I thought, and I told them I was quite impressed. After a discussion of about one hour, they offered me a contract which called for my being the head basketball coach, head baseball coach, assistant football coach, teacher of three classes of biology, and two classes of physical education. There were two problems. First, I had absolutely no experience in biology, except a class I took when I was a sophomore in high school. They were not too concerned about that inexperience and suggested I attempt to stay five pages ahead of the class in my preparation.

The second problem was the salary. The contract was for $2900 per year. I wasn't expecting much, but I was shocked at the limited amount they offered. I politely told them I was certainly interested in the job, but I couldn't even consider it for that amount. They asked me what I thought was more feasible. I then explained that the next afternoon I had an interview at Hailey High School, and the salary there would be $3600 annually. To that they replied, "OK, we will pay you an additional $700 for your coaching assignments, bringing the total to $3600." Inwardly I was very pleased, but tried not to show it. I suggested that they rewrite the contract and let me take it with me to contemplate the offer for a couple of days. They agreed and said they would give me until the following Friday to make a decision.

As I drove from the high school toward the highway, I was very excited. However, there were still two things I wanted to do before I signed any contract. The main thing, of course, was to visit the people at Hailey High School. Prior to that, however, I was going to make an unexpected stop in Boise. During my visit, I had learned that the Payette High School baseball team was playing at Boise High School that same afternoon. I could easily get there for most of the game.

I arrived at the ball park during the third inning. Of course nobody knew who I was, so I was able to get a seat close to the field and study the players in privacy. I was impressed. The Pirates were a very good baseball team with some fine athletes. I made some inquiries of a few Payette fans and found much to my delight that the majority of the better players were only sophomores and juniors.

Before the conclusion of the game I had made a very important decision. I found a public telephone booth and placed a call to the Superintendent of Schools in Hailey, Idaho. When we were connected, I thanked him sincerely for the interest that he had shown in me, but explained that I was going to sign a contract to become the head basketball and baseball coach at Payette High School.

The summer before I had been employed as the life guard and swimming instructor at the Idaho Falls Country Club. For an unmarried college guy that was about as good a summer job as a fellow could ask for. I was to return to the club the next summer as well, but my plans were being changed rapidly.

During my visit to Payette I had been introduced to the head custodian, Mel Debban. Mel was also the coach and general manager of the local semi-pro baseball team, the Payette Packers. He invited me to return to Payette for the summer and catch for the Packers. This would, of course, give me an opportunity to become more familiar with the townspeople and players prior to school opening. Therefore, I found a replacement for me at the I.F. Country Club and left for Payette about the middle of June.

The Payette Packers — 1956.

Mel had suggested I bring a couple of players with me if possible. I talked our ISC third baseman and good friend of mine, LaVoy Sims into spending the summer playing for the Packers as well. LaVoy's nickname was "Flip." Flip talked his younger brother into going also. He was only a sophomore in high school at the time, and we affectionately called him "Flop." Today he is better known as "Duke" Sims. Duke bounced around the major leagues for quite some time after he graduated.

About two or three weeks into the season, Flip and I decided to double-date with a couple of local girls. There were but a few gals in town who were home from college during the summer. Flip and I managed to meet a couple and invited them to go to the game with us one Friday night. Since we had to go to the ball park early for batting practice and infield, we asked the girls to meet us there. After the game we went out to eat.

The next day every high school player in town knew whom I had been with, where we went after the game, and what time I took my date home. That was the first, last, and only time I dated a girl from Payette. I was not about to have my players riding me about my private life. From then on, any courting I would do was going to be in Ontario, Weiser, Caldwell, or Boise.

It seems as if every high school coach gets involved in some sort of school or civic project. I picked a dandy for my initial contribution. As the summer progressed, my thoughts kept going back to the dingy brown floor in the gymnasium. After consulting with Mel Debban and a few other people, I called for a meeting one summer evening of all the students at Payette High School who would be interested in helping to refinish the floor. About seventy students showed up. I challenged each of them to donate one day's pay for materials for the project. Their response was very encouraging.

Mel and I then visited some lumber yards to get the sanding machines, sandpaper, and floor sealant either donated or at cost. Again, the response was positive. Our next move was to solicit volunteer labor from the various service clubs around town. Sanding and re-sealing a gymnasium floor is a very time-consuming piece of work, but our proposal was greeted enthusiastically.

We kicked off the work campaign one Monday evening late in July. We had well over a dozen men stripping and sanding the floor. It was a very difficult job because of the thirty years of old seal to cut through. The first few days we had between eight and twelve volunteers each night, but by the end of the week this dropped drastically to about four to six men. It seemed as if the reality of a long, hard job ahead of us was tempering the enthusiasm quickly. By the middle of the second week, Mel and I were virtually alone. I remember many a long, discouraging night for the two of us until the job was finally completed two and one half weeks later.

The bright, natural grain of the maple floor, freshly painted and sealed, was a beautiful sight. Our civic project had turned into a two-man show, but the finished product made it all worthwhile.

About the first of August a man by the name of Tony Governor approached me with a very tempting offer. Tony was a baseball scout for the St. Louis Cardinals organization. Earlier that summer he had had me and two other Packers "show him our stuff" in a special workout session.

The catcher for the Lewiston Bronco baseball team had unexpectedly jumped the club. They needed a catcher, and they needed him immediately. Tony offered me $100 a week, plus expenses, to leave the next day and finish the six weeks of the season with the Broncos. I was flattered with the offer, and was very tempted to go. I would, however, have had to miss two weeks of football practice and the first week of school. Because it was my "rookie" year as a coach, I just didn't feel that I could accept the invitation. Perhaps there would be another opportunity someday.

Summer passed, and autumn filled the air. Everyone was anxious to get back to school. I was probably the most anxious of all. Our head football coach, Dick Warburton, assigned me to work with the junior varsity football team as well as with the varsity. My fellow coach was one of the biggest characters I have ever known. He was Dale Corn— we called him "Pop." As the year unfolded, Pop Corn and I shared many a laugh and many a tear together. He was also my frosh-soph basketball coach.

On the morning of the first day of classes, Pop and I were discussing student discipline. I expressed my opinion on how to handle serious matters. Pop, who had been teaching and coaching for several years, suggested that I peek through his door window during his first class. It seems as if he had worked out a little ritual to establish classroom decorun.

The bell rang to signal the start of the first hour. Pop and I waited outside the classroom until all of his students were in their seats. He then entered the room, closing the door behind him. I stood outside and watched. A hush fell over the class. Without saying a word, Pop walked to the front of the classroom, took from his pocket a large 6" railroad spike, held the point up against the wall with his left hand, and with one mighty blow drove it into the wall with his right hand. The entire room gasped. (I later found out that Pop had pre-drilled a hole in the wall and covered it with a thin plaster coat.) Without uttering a word, Pop continued. He took off his suit coat, hung it on the spike, rolled up his sleeves, and walked directly to the biggest kid in class. With both hands he grasped the dazed student by the front of his shirt, pulled him up from his desk, shook him fiercely, and slammed him back down in his seat. "Any questions?" Pop asked. He had no disciplinary problems the entire year.

The football season got off to a good start. I didn't know much about what I was doing, but I was enthusiastic. Football was similar to my Biology class—I was just trying to stay a day ahead of the students.

By the end of October our varsity football team had five wins, two losses, and one tie. On the night of November 1, 1956, we were scheduled to play Meridian High School at home. It was to be one of the most eventful days of my life.

Our team was in the locker room in the basement of the gymnasium getting dressed for the game. Pop Corn and I were working side by side taping the ankles of the players. We were having a few laughs with the guys when one of our players who had a reputation of being a little squirrely came rushing in from the hallway and said, "Hey—we'd better get outa here quick, the building's on fire!" Pop and I both quickly reprimanded him for his bad taste of jokes. This was certainly not the time nor place for such a put-on.

Within seconds Dick Warburton entered through the same door. "Get your gear together and get outside quick fellas—this place is full of smoke!" As the players collected their things and scrambled outside, Pop and I started down the hallway toward the furnace room of the main building to see what we could find. Dick was right; the hallway was engulfed in smoke that became more dense as we approached our destination. We were about twenty yards away, when "BOOM," a big explosion sent us reeling. Flames shot from the furnace room. Pop and I made a quick about-face and broke a few sprint records on our way back outside.

The fire trucks drove up just as we got outside. Pop and I helped them get the hoses off. We assumed they would soon have the fire under control, so we took the team back inside for the pre-game briefing. It lasted but a few minutes, and we headed for the game. Once back outside, we could see the flames coming from the roof. We knew then it was going to be serious. Pop and I decided to stay behind to help. One of my basketball players, Ron Coleman, joined us, and we ran around to the front of the building. Most of the fans on the way to the game had stopped. There was a pretty good crowd by then. The firemen were trying to put the ladders to the roof. We met Leo Palumbo and asked what we could do. He had all of the students' records in his office on the middle of the floor. The flames were still confined to the top story. The doors were locked, and Leo didn't have his keys. Pop and I climbed up to his office windows and forced it open. The office was filled with smoke. We climbed in with a flashlight and crept along the floor until we located the file cabinets. We dragged four of them to the window and threw them out. We then climbed back out and closed the window.

The superintendent, Mr. Douglas, met us and asked if we could get to the fire doors that separated the main portion of the building from the junior high school wing. If so, we could probably save the junior high. Pop, Ron Coleman, and I went into the junior high from the west entrance and up to the main floor. We could hardly see for smoke, but we finally found the fire doors and slammed them down. While we were in the junior high section, we decided to get the teachers' record books from each room. We couldn't, however, because we had no keys. No problem, for another student who had joined us whipped out a pocket knife and began to pick each lock for us. In less than five minutes we were out of there with every book.

Our next concern was a great deal of money and some financial records in the safe which was located across the hall from the principal's office. I re-entered Leo's office and opened the door to the hallway to check things out. There was two inches of water on the floor, and plaster from the ceiling was beginning to fall about twenty feet away. I crawled across the hallway and felt the door to the record room. It was cool, so I hollered for Pop and went on in. We found the records immediately and rushed them to the window. We informed Mr. Douglas that we could get to the safe if he wanted to give it a try. He joined us, and we went back across to the record room together. I held the flashlight for Mr. Douglas as he fumbled with the combination to the safe. He was so nervous it took him three times to open it. I wanted to cuss him, but I thought better of it. By then, plaster was beginning to fall around us. We grabbed the money and some other records and got out of there in a hurry.

Payette High School — Before!

During!!

Somebody gave us a report that we were leading Meridian 12-0. We then went down to check the gym. It too was separated from the main building by a fire door. The water, however, had leaked through and onto about twenty feet of the floor. My thoughts quickly flashed to the many hours Mel and I had spent sanding and sealing. We gathered several students together and had them help us sweep the water out, close the doors, and plugged the crack with towels. The fire was at the fire door and we thought our efforts would probably be in vain. By then the fire was really blazing.

We went directly to the athletic equipment room to remove everything we could. Meanwhile, dozens of people were helping to remove power equipment from the shop, appliances from the home economics area, etc. The cooperation was incredible. After about three hours, the fire was under control. The main building had been gutted, but the junior high wing and the gymnasium had been spared.

After!!! My classsroom Monday morning.

The night was not a total loss: we won the ball game 24-18.

Within the week arrangements had been made for all the classes, and school reconvened. The high school students were transferred to the elementary school building which was conveniently located between the gym and the football field. It ended up being a much better facility than the one we were in. The junior high students set up classes in the local Armory. The elementary grades were moved to several churches around town.

Basketball practice was to begin November 15, but before we could get started about one-half of the gym floor had to be replaced. The water that had leaked onto it during the fire had caused considerable warpage. Fortunately, insurance paid for the replacement. Once again my thoughts went back to the many hours of sanding during the summer. Had we not refinished the floor, they probably would have replaced the entire thing.

After two short weeks of practice we played our first home game against Mountain Home. They used a 1-2-2 zone the entire game. We attacked it with the 1-3-1 zone offense we used at Idaho State. I can still see the headlines in the newspaper the next day. PIRATES PASS BALL BEAUTIFULLY—BUT FORGOT TO SHOOT. We were beaten 44 to 28. The paper was right. We passed the ball around the perimeter all night long, but seldom penetrated the zone for internal shots. My players simply had not been adequately prepared to attack the zone. I had an uneasy sense of self-realization that perhaps I didn't know as much about this game of basketball as I thought I did. I didn't like the feeling.

I was to receive my first technical foul the next weekend. It was during a game at Fruitland, a small town located five miles west of Payette. Earlier that year I had met and was dating the homecoming queen from the College of Idaho. She was from Fruitland, and as irony would have it, her younger brother was a starting guard for their team. I invited her to be my guest at the game. She accepted and sat in the stands with her mother.

The first half we scored a grand total of one field goal and nine free throws. We went into the dressing room behind—something like 32-11. My career was in its infant stages, and already I **was feeling** some emotions of greater magnitude than I was accustomed to: embarrassment, frustration, anger and helplessness. I was so upset at halftime that instead of diagramming plays on the blackboard, I was breaking off pieces of chalk and throwing them at the players. Surely they were wondering what kind of maniac Palumbo had hired.

The second half got worse before it got better. About three minutes into the half the ref called a bad one. I stood up in protest, turned around, and kicked my bench. 'Bout broke my toe. The ref quickly planted a "T" on me. I deserved it. Nevertheless, I was convinced he was the only guy in the house having a worse night than me. To make matters worse, he had my date's brother shoot the technical foul shot at *our* basket. He missed—but never mind. I walked right out onto the floor and confronted the official. Would you believe that there I was, standing toe to toe with the ref at the free throw line? The crowd was going nuts. "You don't know what you're doing, do ya?" I challenged.

"Whatta ya mean?"

"You just shot the "T" at our basket!"

"Then we'll try it again at the other basket!" With that he turned from me and started toward the Fruitland basket.

"You can't do that," I protested. As I reached out to stop him, I grabbed his striped shirt and pulled it completely out of his pants. Even I couldn't believe what I had done. He was so shocked he didn't even call a second "T" on me as I stumbled back to my seat. The crowd was in stitches, cheering me like crazy, even though it was a Fruitland crowd. I just sat there in disbelief the rest of the game. We lost 54-33.

"You just shot the "T" at our basket!"

My date was waiting for me in the lobby after I had dismissed the players. Not knowing exactly what to say, I started with, "Would you like to go get something to eat?"

"I'm sorry, but I believe you had better take me straight home," she replied.

"Was it that bad?" I pleaded.

"Bad? My mother has instructed me that I may never go out with you again."

That ended that romance.

The next few days I had cause for serious contemplation. We were 0-2. My enthusiasm and positive self-assurance had received a couple of blows. As painful as it was to admit, certain facts were suddenly quite obvious. I didn't know nearly as much about the game of basketball as I thought I did, and I wasn't teaching what I did know very effectively.

I subsequently made two important decisions. First, I would discontinue teaching my players all the exotic plays we had used at ISC. I wasn't coaching, I was over-coaching by simply copying the only concepts I had ever learned in basketball. We needed to get back to the basics. Second, from that day on I would read and study at least one article per day pertaining to basketball techniques and strategies. My knowledge of this great game was too limited, and I needed to broaden my scope considerably. With the exception of the time I spent in the military, I studied an article per day for the next several years.

Slowly the program started to turn. We were beginning to play reasonably well and win a good portion of our games. I was inwardly pleased with my personal progress as a coach. It seemed that each day I learned something new. I learned much through experiencing the ups and downs of coaching.

Twice a week Pop Corn and I would join a few other guys from town and drive to Weiser, Idaho, to play in their recreation basketball league. One of our teammates was a recent graduate and former great athlete from Payette High School. His name was Harmon Killebrew. Harmon had just completed his rookie year as a bonus baby for the Washington Senators. He would often tell me in the car on the way to the games that he was confident that he could hit major league pitching if the Senators would only give him a chance to play regularly. The only pitcher he felt could give him trouble was Whitey Ford of the Yankees. Harmon's career is now history. He ended up being one of the all-time great homerun hitters in major league baseball. He was a pretty fair country basketball player, too.

During the second round of league play we were scheduled to play Meridian again. This time the game was at Meridian. We had previously beaten them quite handily at our place.

Their home court at that time was extremely small. Instead of the regulation size of 84 by 50 feet, their floor measured approximately 74 by 40 feet. The narrow court helped make the 1-2-2 zone they employed that evening very effective. Fortunately, our defense was also excellent. At halftime Meridian led the low scoring game 22-20.

I felt we had to get them out of their zone if we expected to win. Therefore, I elected to do something I had not done previously as a coach and have seldom done since. We were going to stall as soon as we tied the score or got the lead. It was my hope that stalling tactics would force them to play us man-to-man.

We got the tip at halftime and scored. It was 22-22. As good fortune would have it, we rebounded their first missed shot and promptly went into the stall. There was no five second rule or any other rule to speed up play in those days. Instead of changing to man-to-man, Meridian chose to sit back in their zone and let us hold onto the ball. We stood motionless with it for the next seven minutes. We missed the last second shot and the third quarter ended in a tie.

We controlled the tip to begin the fourth quarter and went directly to the stall once again. After three or four minutes Meridian reluctantly changed to a man-to-man defense. Within seconds we scored a field goal to take the lead 24-22. Our game plan was working. We traded a few baskets and then with seven seconds to play they fouled us intentionally. It was a two-shot foul. We were ahead by three points. With the clock stopped, our player stepped to the line and made both free throws. We led by five points 31 to 26. I sat back and heaved a sigh of relief—we were but seven seconds away from victory. What happened next would qualify for Ripley's "Believe it or not." I was about to learn a lesson I have never forgotten.

They passed the ball inbounds to their guard, who dribbled the length of the floor virtually unmolested within three seconds and made a layup. It was 31 to 28. My player took it out of bounds. Instead of holding it out of bounds until time expired, he panicked and attempted a hurried pass to a teammate. A Meridian player intercepted the pass and drove for the layup. We could have allowed him to make the basket and still won, but oh no! We fouled him as he shot the ball. The basket was good—a 2 and 1 attempt. With no time on the clock they made the free throw to tie the game 31-31. Five points had been scored in seven seconds.

We went into overtime, and Meridian won 35 to 33. Since that day I have drilled my team considerably on last second situations. Within the next few years my team won two separate games in last second situations that were more incredible than the meridian game.

The regular season ended, and we went to the District tournament. At the tourney we beat Weiser and Meridian and lost to Mountain Home and Boise, good for fourth place. We won the sportsmanship trophy, coming a long way since the game at Fruitland.

After the season we put the basketballs away and broke out the bats—it was time for baseball season. For several years Payette had enjoyed the reputation of being one of the finest baseball teams in the state of Idaho. My high school team lived up to that reputation. We won 14 consecutive games, beating most of the biggest and best teams in the state. We lost to Nampa in the state tournament and finished the season with a 21/4 record..

Introducing the players at the Athletic Awards Banquet.

Halfway through the baseball season I received a letter from Uncle Sam requesting that I go to Boise to take a physical examination for induction into the U.S. Army. Late in April I did so and passed with flying colors. They informed me that in thirty days I would receive my induction papers for a two-year stint in the Army. I was not too excited about that.

I made some quick inquiries and found that the Air Force Reserve still had one slot available for candidates from the Idaho region. To qualify for this six-month active duty program I would have to pass a test and compete with other applicants from the region. I took the test and was fortunate enough to be the final candidate selected.

My orders were cut in advance. On August 28, 1957, I was to report to Lackland Air Force Base in San Antonio, Texas, to begin basic training for a six-month hitch in the U.S. Air Force Reserves.

I handed my letter of resignation to Leo Palumbo about the first of May. It had been a wonderful experience, and I regretted having to leave, but I had no choice. I then contacted Tony Governor, the scout for the St. Louis Cardinals. Since I didn't have to report until late August, I was anxious to try my hand at professional baseball. He suggested I contact Sib Kleffner, the owner of the Boise Braves. Sib and I had been acquainted for several years. He expressed a strong interest in my playing for the Braves and asked me to report to the baseball stadium the day school let out to sign a contract for the summer.

Payette had been very good to me, the year was complete, and my future was set for the next nine months. School was released at 12 noon Friday in late May. By 1 p.m. I was in my car heading for Boise.

4

CLIMBING
THE LADDER

I ate, I sat, and I thought. It had taken me only an hour to drive to Boise. After a quick lunch I sat and waited for 5:00 p.m. to roll around so I could go to the Braves Stadium to meet Sib Kleffner. The longer I sat, the more I thought about my future. Did I really want to spend the summer playing pro baseball? How good was I? How far could I go? What would I do when I got out of the Air Force? I figured it would be difficult for me to get a good basketball coaching position upon my discharge. Chances would obviously be much better if I went back to graduate school and worked toward a master's degree. BYU—that's where I could go. I had been impressed with that school ever since that cold December day three years earlier when Paul Tueller and I spent two days in Provo.

A pivotal point in my life was about to occur. Why wait, I wondered. I was confident I could bounce around some in the minor leagues, but I was realistic enough to know that I would never make the big leagues. Why not start graduate school right now this summer before I had to report for active duty? Another very important decision was made in Boise.

At 4:00 p.m. I called Sib Kleffner and thanked him for his interest and courtesy, but I was going to Brigham Young University to enroll in the graduate program.

I drove to Pocatello and spent the night with my parents. The next morning Mom washed all my clothes. I packed my bags again and headed for Provo. This time I made the trip in 4 1/2 hours instead of the eight it had taken Paul and me.

My Aunt Alice (Palfreyman) had a student apartment in her basement that was vacant for the summer, so I hung my hat there.

It was a great summer. I started working toward my Master of Science degree with a major in physical education and a minor in recreation. It was my first experience with summer school, and I enjoyed it immeasurably. I played softball two nights a week and baseball two nights a week. I met many new people and created life-

long friendships. The most important event of the summer occurred
the day I met a young lady by the name of Bee Wright. Eighteen
months later we were married for time and all eternity in the Salt
Lake City Temple of The Church of Jesus Christ of Latter-day Saints.
It was the third and final of the three most important decisions of my
life. It has been, without reservation, the most important and wisest
decision of all.

Bee and I double-dating during summer school at BYU 1957.

   Summer terminated, and on August 28, 1957, I left for Lackland
Air Force Base in San Antonio, Texas, to begin my six months of
active duty in the USAF Reserves. It was a period of time that I would
not want to trade for any other six-month period of my life, yet I would
not have wanted to spend one day longer than required.
   I was picked up at the airport by a short, blond, steel-gray eyed
sergeant who was to be my TI (training instructor). In my initial efforts
to be friendly and get acquainted, I quickly discovered that military life
was going to be far different than civilian life. The TI wanted nothing
to do with a man-to-man or personal relationship. It was to be strictly
a dictator-(TI) to-raw-boot-camp-trainee (me) arrangement.
   As we drove to the barracks he asked me where I came from and
what I did. I explained that I had graduated from college and had just

finished my first year as a high school basketball coach. Upon hearing this, he informed me that he was appointing me as the Flight Commander until someone came along that was more suitable for the job. (I later found out that a Flight consisted of 40 airmen under the jurisdiction of a TI. The Flight Commander was one of the airmen who was, in effect, to be their "student leader.")

When we arrived at the barracks we discovered that there had been an error in my pre-cut orders, and that I had arrived one day earlier than the other 39 airmen. I was, therefore, the only guy in the barracks for the next 24 hours, with the exception of the barracks guard. To my delight, I found that the Flight Commander had the privilege of two mattresses on a single bunk rather than the regular double-deck bunk beds and single mattresses that the other airmen were to sleep on. It was then and there that I determined that nobody was going to take the Flight Commander job away from me.

I sat alone in the barracks for the rest of the day. At 8:55 p.m. an announcement came over the loud speaker system: "At 9:00 lights will be out, all airmen will be in bed, and there will be no more talking." I quickly changed to my pajamas, hung up my clothes, and then, as had been my life-long custom knelt by the side of my bunk to say my prayers and thank my Father in Heaven for the blessings of that day.

The next day the remaining 39 airmen arrived. They were from all walks of life, races and religions. The day was spent in orientation and getting acquainted. At 8:55 p.m. that evening the noise level in our open bay barracks with all forty airmen near their respective bunks was broken with the same announcement: "At 9:00 lights will be out, all airmen will be in bed, and there will be no more talking." Once again I changed to my pajamas and hung up my clothing. As I started to kneel by the side of my bunk to offer my prayers, I felt extremely uncomfortable. I was embarrassed and frankly afraid to kneel in front of the other airmen. Instead, I quietly slipped into bed and waited for lights-out. I spent a very restless night, ashamed of myself for not having the courage to honor my religious conviction because of self-imposed peer pressure.

The following day was spent much the same as the second: More orientation, some drills, and getting acquainted. Evening came and at 8:55 p.m. we once again heard the familiar announcement: "At 9:00 p.m. lights will be out. . . ." This time I was determined to be true to my faith. When I knelt by the side of my bunk, the noise level of the airmen chattering and joking as they got ready for bed was very high. I was very self-conscious as I began my prayers. As I continued, however, a hush slowly but surely filled the barracks. Instead of the boisterous volume, there was at best a subdued murmur. When I finished my prayers, I slowly stood and looked about the open bay. There were at least twenty other airmen kneeling in prayer. The rest of the men were very quietly hanging up their clothing while respecting the solemn moment their buddies chose to spend with their Father in Heaven.

From that moment on, our Flight became a very close group. At the end of our four weeks of basic training, we were voted as Most Outstanding Flight at Lackland Air Force Base.

After a big nite on the town in   *Writing to Bee.*
Wichita Falls.   *Sheppard AFB, 1957.*

Basketball re-entered my life shortly after being transferred to Sheppard AFB in Wichita Falls, Texas. I was assigned to Sheppard from late September to early November, at which time I would be sent to Travis AFB, located between San Francisco and Sacramento, California.

Tryouts for the base basketball team were given about the middle of October. I was successful in making the base team, at which time the officer in charge of special services asked me to have my orders changed to remain with the team until the completion of the basketball season. That would have meant staying in Texas until the end of March, an extra month in the Reserves. I said thanks, but no thanks. I much preferred going to California and playing for the base team at Travis.

When I arrived at Travis AFB in mid-November, however, I was disappointed to find that they had no base team as such. There was merely an intramural program, with an all-star team to be picked in February to represent the base at a Strategic Air Command (SAC) tournament in Spokane, Washington.

Therefore, I spent the next three months playing intramural basketball and refereeing in various leagues. I had been assigned to the VIP section of Passenger Flight Control. I worked the graveyard shift from 11 p.m. to 7 a.m. It was my responsibility to assist Bird Colonels and Generals on flights to and from the Pacific Theater. It was a great job, and allowed me to have my evenings free to play and referee. I also played for the LDS M-Men team in Fairfield, California, a small town just outside the base.

The first week in February I was picked as a player-coach for the all-star team we sent to the SAC Tourney in Spokane. The tournament was only a four-day affair, but at its conclusion there was a series of snowstorms of such magnitude that we were "socked in" for an additional two weeks. By the time weather permitted us to return to Travis, I was only six days away from being discharged. I spent that last week processing out and saying goodbye to my close friends.

I was discharged on February 28, 1958, and returned to Provo to continue work on my M.S. degree at BYU. I was awarded a graduate assistantship to teach a couple of classes of tennis for the P.E. Department. That, coupled with a full academic load, baseball two nights a week, and softball two nights a week, kept me quite busy during the spring and summer quarters. I did find time, however, to become engaged to Bee, and on August 22, 1958, we were married.

For time and all eternity.

As good fortune would have it, I had been hired to teach and coach at the Brigham Young University Laboratory School (BY High) right in Provo. My assignment was challenging. I was to teach junior high school math (the school included kindergarten through high school), high school physical education, and to serve as assistant football, head basketball, head baseball and head tennis coach. The only other coach on our staff was Jed Gibson, a former great University of Utah football player. He was the head football, assistant basketball, head wrestling, and head track and field coach. Between the two of us, we handled every sport in the school—and then some.

The BY High coaching staff — Jed Gibson and me.

BY High was housed at the original Brigham Young Academy buildings, and we practiced in the gymnasium on the third story of a building built in 1906. The floor was far inferior to the one at Payette. A balcony hung over one end, an equipment storage room extended two feet onto one corner of the court, and old-fashioned steam-heat radiators surrounded the floor on three sides.

Teaching Marion Bentley a fake and drive at the BYH practice gym

Our games, however, were played in the BYU Smith Fieldhouse, which had a seating capacity of 11,000. Our 400-500 fans per game didn't make much of a dent.

My first years at BY High provided two wins that paralleled, if not exceeded, the Payette-Meridian game I explained earlier. The first occurred at the BYU Fieldhouse in a game against Judge Memorial High School of Salt Lake City. Judge was coached by one of my oldest friends, Steve Detmer. Steve and I had attended school together in Pocatello from the fifth grade on. In fact, it was Steve that talked me into playing my first game at Washington Elementary School when we were in the sixth grade.

With one second remaining in the game, we fouled Judge Memorial. They were ahead by one point at the time, and they were granted a one-and-one free throw situation. The Judge players were ecstatic, and their bench began to celebrate. But they were premature.

The Judge player missed the first free throw, our inside player rebounded and turned to throw the ball the length of the court in a last-ditch, desperate attempt to score. Another Judge player instinctively raised his hands to block the attempt, and as our player released the ball, whacked him across the arm. Would you believe that the referee blew his whistle and called a foul? That, of course, was bad news enough for Judge, but things went from bad to worse when the ref further called it a "shooting" foul, and awarded us two shots. I buried my head in my hands and thought to myself, "Welcome to Provo, Steve." We made both free throws and won the game by one point.

The 1962 BY High Wildcats.

An even more astonishing finish occurred in a game at Richfield High School. Throughout the contest the score was tied, or we took turns exchanging the lead. With but seconds to play, Richfield scored a field goal to take a three-point lead. The seconds ticked away 3...2...1. Bob Martin, our big red-headed forward threw up a desperation shot and was fouled in the act. The timer stopped the clock on the referee's whistle. The scoreboard registered 0:00, but the horn had not sounded. There was a mere fraction of one second to play. As soon as the timer flipped the switch back on, the horn would sound and the game would be over.

I had already started down the sidelines to congratulate the Richfield coach. When it was apparent that the game was not officially over, I retreated to our bench and summoned a time out. In the huddle I laid out our strategy. We had maybe one chance in a hundred of winning, but we were going to give it a try.

In the locker room after a 64-59 victory in a playoff game against Pleasant Grove for a berth in the State Tournament

The team took their respective positions along the free throw lane. Bob stood at the line, and with his sure left hand calmly made the first free throw. So far, so good. We were now only two points behind. The referee handed him the ball for the second attempt. All eyes were glued on the rim. Bob dribbled the ball once, twice, three times, and then lofted a soft looping shot toward the basket. It was picture perfect, just as we had planned. The ball struck the front edge of the rim and rebounded directly back toward Bob. As soon as it hit the rim, Bob lunged across the free throw line, jumped high into the air, and got his big left hand under the ball. The horn sounded as he tipped it upward toward the basket once again. The ball bounced around the rim. If it fell through it would be ruled good, because Bob was considered in the act of shooting when the horn sounded. Lady Luck was good to us once again. The ball finally rolled into the basket. Two points—the score was tied. We had forced the game into overtime.

The three points that we scored with no time remaining on the clock seemed to take all the fire out of the Richfield team. The next three minutes belonged to the blue and gold-clad Wildcats, and we won the game handily in the overtime.

I have often repeated this experience to my players to impress upon them the importance of two things: (1) a free throw shooter must always be blocked off after his attempt and (2) the game is never over until the final horn has sounded.

During the summer of 1960 I was involved in an incident with a Peeping Tom that is one of the all-time classics in Provo. Merrill Hardy, a dear friend and former softball and baseball teammate and I were returning home late one Friday evening from the Utah State Softball Tournament in Murray. It was nearly 1 a.m. as we drove east on 820 North toward my residence. About three blocks from my house we passed a young man dressed in Army khaki fatigues and black gym shoes. I assumed he was walking home after a late date. I thought to myself what a strange outfit he was wearing for a date. I didn't give it another thought, however.

Merrill dropped me off at my home, we said good night, and I went inside to greet my wife, Bee. She had been cleaning the house while waiting up for me. We talked about the game for awhile, and then decided to retire for the evening. Since I was still in my game uniform, Bee suggested that she shower first while I read the evening paper, then I could shower. When she went into the bathroom, I took off my uniform and pulled a pair of clean under garments halfway on to sit on the bed and read the paper.

As I awaited my turn to shower, I heard some dogs barking towards the back of the house. Earlier that day Bee and I had discovered a very young kitten in rather poor health in some bushes by our house. I had made a little bed for it on our back patio/porch as we attempted to nurse it back to good health. I assumed when I heard the dogs bark that they might be molesting the kitten. I set the paper down and with one hand holding up my loose-fitting, half-on under garments walked toward the back door which was located in our kitchen.

Our house was located on a corner lot. The entrance was on the north side, and the back patio/porch was adjacent to our kitchen and bathroom on the south side of the house. It was an elevated porch, surrounded with a wrought iron fence and covered with an aluminum patio roof. To get onto the porch one had to walk up our car driveway, back walkway, up three steps and enter at the southwest corner. Kitty-corner from the entrance/exit in the northeast corner of the porch we had a bench about two feet high that we kept potted plants on. In the middle of the porch we had a table and chair. The kitchen door led directly onto the porch.

As I approached the door I glanced to my left and saw out of the kitchen window a very unexpected sight. In the corner of the porch the lights from the bathroom window revealed the face of a husky, dark wavy-haired man. I must have been a very trusting person, because the first thing that entered my mind was what a strange time of night it was for the utility department to have a man reading the electric meter. No sooner had that thought crossed my mind when I realized that the face, in fact, belonged to a Peeping Tom who had walked up my driveway, climbed the steps to the porch, then climbed onto the bench in the corner of the porch in an attempt to peek through the bathroom window at my wife showering. Fortunately, the window was opaque and impossible to see through.

I slowly opened the kitchen door and took one step onto the porch. "Hey you!" I challenged. The man was startled and obviously frightened. He was like a scared dog cornered, because I was seething with anger by then. He slowly stepped down off the bench. I took another calculated step onto the porch. He stepped behind the table to keep us separated. Suddenly, he bolted to his left for the exit from the porch. I quickly lunged to my right and met him at the opening. I tackled him around the shoulders and knocked him down the steps to the walkway. We wrestled on the walk for a moment, and then he broke free. I lunged at him again, and knocked him through a wooden fence separating my house from the neighbor. In the struggle my under garments were torn quite badly. He broke loose again and started running north, up the grass on the west side of my house. Half naked, I made a flying tackle and knocked him down for the third time. This time I quickly climbed on his back. With my left hand, I was trying to get a hammer lock under his arm and over the back of his neck, and with my right hand trying to get my under garments up. I finally succeeded in doing both. All this time I was hollering at the top of my lungs for my neighbors. "Burt!" "Jim!" "Bee– call the police!" "Rex!" "Belmont!"

I remember his shoulders being so wide I had a hard time getting a hammer lock on him. I was so incensed with anger I didn't even think about fear at the time. When I finally got him under control I grabbed his long, wavy hair with my left hand, twisted his face, and hit him with all my power with my right fist. "Peek at my wife, will ya?" I said, then traded places with my right hand, held his hair, and belted him with my left fist. About this moment the first neighbor arrived on the scene. It was Vivian Anderson (the mother of Belmont and Greg Anderson— both former BYU players). When she saw me hitting this guy, she ordered me, "Frank Arnold, will you please get off that poor boy and put some pants on." "Vivian," I retaliated, "will you please be quiet and go get me some pants." I had punched the poor guy into complete submission when the second neighbor showed up. He took off his belt, wrapped it around his fist, and then stalked the gasping Tom first left and then right, and then said, "O.K., fella, now there's two of us." At the time all I could think of was, "Thanks a lot friend! Where were you when I really needed help?"

Within minutes it seemed like the entire neighborhood showed up. Two police cars arrived, one with two uniformed officers and one with a plain-clothes man. Vivian brought me some pants from Bee, whom I later found out had been so frightened she ran from the shower, locked all the doors, and called the police. Luckily, the guy didn't start chasing me, and I didn't have to get into the house in a hurry.

The two uniformed policemen took the Tom to the emergency room of the hospital to have him checked over. In my anger I had given him a pretty severe beating. The other policeman took me directly to the police station to sign a complaint and await the others so they could book him.

After a wait of well over an hour, the two uniformed officers embarrassingly walked into the station. "Frank," they asked, "did you happen to get the name of the Peeping Tom?" "No, fellas, I really didn't have an opportunity to ask him," I replied. "Where in the devil is he?"

The Tom had been strapped to the emergency ward table waiting for the doctor to arrive to treat him. He had had a fractured jaw, broken nose, and facial lacerations. One officer had gone to the restroom, the other had followed the nurse into another area to assist her with some supplies. In their absence, the Tom had unstrapped himself and walked away. To this day no one knows who he was or where he is.

I have often been asked by young coaches what a person has to do to get the opportunity to coach at the collegiate level. There is no simple answer. One certainly has to be prepared. Preparedness comes through many hours of study, dedication, and hard work. Unfair as it may seem, however, a good number of job opportunities come about because of two things: timing and contacts.

It seems as if a person needs to be fortunate enough to be in the right place at the right time. He must also know somebody who can assist him in "getting his foot into the door." Once the door is open for him his ability and his preparedness will determine whether or not he will be successful in obtaining or maintaining the position.

There is no doubt in my mind that I am coaching at the collegiate level today because of a unique stroke of luck. It opened a door for me. Once I got my foot in that door, however, I feel I have been able to step inside and continue to progress because of an unwavering dedication and relentless pursuit of self-improvement. I am still not satisfied with my personal accomplishments and will not be until I have reached certain goals that will always remain confidential. When I reach those goals, I will redefine and re-establish new goals and priorities in my life to pursue.

The stroke of luck came on day in May of 1961. There was a head basketball position open at Nampa High School in Nampa, Idaho. I applied for the job and was selected as one of the finalists to be granted an interview. Bee and I drove from Provo to Nampa one weekend in May. Our route took us through Twin Falls, Idaho. As we were driving through Twin Falls we passed a man walking down a sidewalk smoking his pipe. It was Steve Belko, my former coach at Idaho State College. Steve had since been appointed as the head basketball coach at the University of Oregon. I hadn't seen him for over five years.

We made a quick U-turn and I jumped out to greet Steve. He and his wife Kathy were visiting her parents who lived in Twin Falls. As we exchanged pleasantries, I explained that we were on our way to Nampa to interview for a job. I further explained that although I was enjoying my experiences at BY High, I hoped to find a coaching job at a bigger school that would offer me new challenges and opportunities.

As we parted, he made a comment to me that eventually altered my coaching career. He suggested, "If you don't get the position at

Nampa, why don't you consider coming to Eugene and being a graduate assistant coach for me at the University of Oregon?" I was pleased and honored that he had proposed such an opportunity to me, but I really didn't give it serious consideration at the time.

I was not hired at Nampa, and so returned to BY High for my fourth year. As usual, I enjoyed the players and the personal association at BY High, but as the year progressed I became more and more anxious to seek bigger and better coaching opportunities. Belko's proposal kept coming back to me. One evening Bee and I, after several days of contemplation, decided to make a move. I wrote Belko and asked him if the invitation was still open. He responded positively. Therefore, I applied for an early sabbatical leave from BY High. We decided to spend the next year at the University of Oregon, working toward an Ed.D degree in physical education, while assisting Coach Belko in the basketball program. I was to receive no remuneration for helping coach basketball, so our entire income was to be from our sabbatical leave income of one-half salary. (I believe it was about $2400.) It was with great sacrifice that Bee and I and our two children, Kelly (age 2 1/2) and Kris (age 4 months) headed for Eugene in August 1962.

We fell in love with Eugene immediately. It was a beautiful city with beautiful people. I doubt if I have ever spent a more demanding year in my entire life. I usually left our apartment about 7 a.m. and didn't return until 11 p.m. I was taking a full academic load working on my doctorate degree plus assisting the basketball program full-time. Although I was not paid, I also taught Coach Belko's basketball theory class for P.E. majors. I spent at least four to five hours per day with different responsibilities in basketball. I did very little recruiting, however. I simply did not have the time. When I was not in class or on the basketball floor, I was in the library. I believe I was able to schedule about two hours per week for my family, excluding Sundays.

As the year progressed, Coach Belko gave me more and more responsibility until I was eventually making some trips with the team and getting my feet wet in the new world of recruiting. I remember being sent to a small town in Washington once to watch a seven footer. The opposition stalled the entire game, however, so I only saw him take two shots all night. I was afraid Belko would be mad at me because I couldn't honestly tell him how good the prospect was.

Bee was fortunate enough to get a part-time job teaching a couple of classes in Child Development at Oregon State University (she had her M.S. in Child Development from BYU). Every other day, therefore, she drove the 45 miles to Corvallis and back. I was a UO Duck and she was a OSU Beaver. Our friends had some fun with us over that arrangement.

Basketball season ended, and our financial situation was becoming critical. Our car engine had "blown up" on one of Bee's return trips. We had to buy another car that we couldn't afford. I eventually got a job making sewer drainage pipes for $2.27/hour. I worked four hours a day in place of the basketball time allocation. It also seemed like it would never stop raining. We were both getting very tired and depressed.

Coach Belko had made a recommendation to hire me full-time the following year, but it was declined. The current athletic director didn't feel that the program could afford a full-time assistant. I did not want to return to BY High, but there were not many alternative coaching opportunities available. The BY High officials were anxious to know of my intentions. They sent me a contract to return as the head basketball coach. After considerable deliberation Bee and I decided to return it unsigned along with a letter of resignation.

We were jobless, but I felt at peace with myself and confident that we had made the correct decision. Less than a week had gone by when I was contacted by some authorities at Pocatello High School, my alma mater. The head coaching job was vacant, and they wanted to know if I would consider the opening. Our prayers had been answered. Pocatello had been without question the finest basketball school in the state of Idaho for the past several years. It was a big step forward.

We accepted the job, the contract was signed, we packed our bags, and headed for Pocatello.

The Pocatello Indians had won or taken no less than second in the state for seven consecutive years. The high school had become so overcrowded, however, that the school district had just completed the new Highland High School, so the student body (and athletic teams) were to be split in half. It made little difference, because only two lettermen returned from the previous state championship team.

There was a definite reason for the success Poky High had been enjoying in basketball. The city had one of the finest feeder programs established that any high school could ask for. The senior high school was fed by students from Franklin Junior High, Irvine Junior High, and the new Alameda Junior High. Each Junior High school had seventh, eighth and ninth grade teams, each with individual coaches. All of the junior high school coaches were hired by the city athletic director, Byron Toone. They were hired with the understanding that they were to report directly to the senior high head coach. Poky High also had sophomore, and junior varsity teams.

All nine of the junior high school coaches, the sophomore coach, and the JV coach met with the varsity coach once a month to review the total city basketball program. The junior high coaches were allowed to teach their own offense, but they were required to teach the fundamental skills and defense as dictated by the varsity coach. Each team had a seventeen game schedule and was allowed to zone no more than three times per year. It was a great development program.

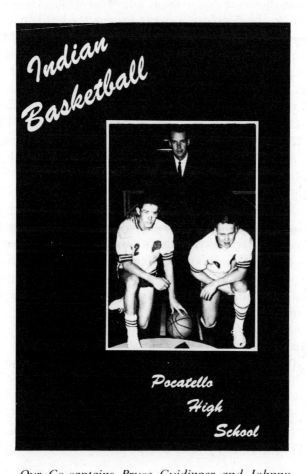

Our Co-captains Bruce Guidinger and Johnny Carlyle.

The addition of Highland High School necessitated the splitting of students from some of the junior high schools, so the program was no longer quite as pure. Nevertheless, the continuity of the program was far greater than most cities ever enjoy.

Our season was rather average and went without any significant happenings. At the conclusion of the season, the head coach at Idaho State University, Jim Nau, called me and asked if I would like to drive with him to Eugene to see the NCAA Far West regionals in March. I was anxious to do so, for it would allow me to see some of my old friends, as well as the tournament. Our principal, however, was reluctant to give me three days off. My desire to go was greater than my common sense. On Wednesday morning, I did something I had never done before, and have never done since. I had Bee call the school and inform them that I was sick in bed. Actually, Jim and I had left the night before for Eugene.

The tourney was great. I saw my old friends, got a lead on a new job possibility, and headed home. On Friday, I started feeling kind of weak and began to cough quite regularly. By the time we got home late Saturday night, I felt awful. Early Sunday morning I went to the emergency room of the Bannock Memorial Hospital to have a doctor look me over. They took some chest x-rays and determined that I had bronchial pneumonia. I was sent directly upstairs and checked into a room for treatment.

On Monday morning, my wife called the school for the fourth consecutive day and reported me sick. Later that day I had an unexpected visitor, our principal Dr. C. H. Teuscher. "Frank," he said. "I have an apology to make to you. When your wife called in Wednesday to report your being sick, I really didn't believe her. I honestly thought you were faking so that you could attend the tournament in Eugene. I can see now that I was wrong. Will you please forgive me?" I graciously (and sheepishly) accepted his apology.

While I was in Eugene I visited with "Skeets" O'Connell, the head basketball coach and athletic director at Clark College (a junior college) in Vancouver, Washington. "Skeets" was a tall red-headed Irishman and one of the finest men I have ever associated with. He had recently had surgery for varicose veins, and his doctor was concerned that he may not be able to withstand the rigors of coaching two to three hours per day on a hardwood floor. "Skeets" asked me if I would be interested in joining him at Clark College as his assistant, with the strong possibility that I would be appointed as head coach before the season got underway.

Bee and I discussed the proposal at length and decided it would be a great opportunity to get back into coaching at the collegiate level. We felt it would be a good stepping stone to bigger and better things.

We moved to Vancouver in September of 1964. "Skeets" resigned his basketball position that same summer, so I was appointed as head coach prior to the opening day of school. I also coached tennis and taught a few activity classes and some professional classes for P.E. majors.

Clark was a community college, and by design the student body was made up primarily of students from the local community in and around Vancouver. The recruitment of basketball players, however, was more widespread. Our starting lineup ended up consisting of a center from Nome, Alaska; two forwards from Portland and Chicago; and two guards from Los Angeles and Newark, New Jersey. Each recruit was a story in and of itself, but the most interesting was our guard from Newark, Richard "Magic" Taylor.

Midway through the summer I received a call from the head coach at the University of Idaho, Jim Goddard. He asked me if I had need of a super ball-handling guard. He knew of one on the east coast, but had no financial assistance available and was hoping to place him at a J.C. I assured him that we would be interested and able to give him some financial aid. Jim said he would have the player call me within the week.

About 10 p.m. the following evening I received a collect call from Newark. "Coach—this is "Magic" Taylor. I'm at the airport, my plane leaves in three minutes; I'll arrive in Portland at 3:15 a.m., pick me up!" He hung up. I didn't even have a chance to say hello or goodbye.

The Portland Airport was just across the Columbia River from Vancouver. I got out of bed at 2 a.m. and drove to the terminal to wait for my new guard, "Magic". Needless to say, I was very curious to see what kind of a person and player he would be.

When the plane arrived, several persons exited that were obviously not athletic types. Then this young Black man walked off the jetway with a style all his own. He was dressed in a three-piece white suit, black shirt, white tie, white shoes, and white panama hat. He had a black cape over his shoulders, cheerfully whistling while twirling a black umbrella around his finger as he peered through his sun glasses looking for a friendly face. It had to be "Magic".

I introduced myself to him and was greeted with a hand shake and a slap on the back that almost knocked me over. "Hey Coach—good to meet cha man, let's get it on!" We picked up his luggage, jumped in the

Denny Huston and I conferring at Clark College...

"Magic" Taylor seated to my left.

"You gotta be kidding!"

"Oh my gosh!"

car, and headed for Vancouver. Magic was one non-stop chatterbox, shooting questions and statements at me like a rapid-fire machine gun. I was going to like this effervescent guy.

"What cha think of the rabbit, coach?"

"The what?"

"The rabbit, man, the rabbit! You know, the bunny."

"Richard, I'm afraid I don't know who you're talking about."

"Ah, coach—the bunny, Elgin—Elgin Baylor—How'd ya like his 30 foot springer?"

"His what?"

"His thirty foot springer, man; you know jump shot from thirty feet; that's my favorite shot, too."

"You shoot jump shots from thirty feet?"

"Yeah man," he slapped me across the knee and about sent the accelerator through the floor board. "I'm deadly at thirty."

"I gotta see this," I thought to myself.

"What kinda defense ya like coach?"

"I prefer to play pressure man-to-man."

"Nose-to-nose? Put it to 'em for 94? Yea man—we's gonna get along jes fine."

There was about ten seconds of uncharacteristic silence, and then he asked rather inquisitively, "Coach, don't cha kinda wonder why they call me 'Magic'?"

"Well, 'Magic'," I replied, "I rather expect it's because you're such a fine ball-handler."

"Yea, man," he shouted with glee. "I can do it, man, I can really do it—you'll see—you're gonna like my style."

He had me exhausted by the time I got him to his apartment. I had him rooming with another player from Chicago, Bill Wilkeson. Bill was the exact opposite of "Magic", poised, polished and articulate. They would make a great pair.

The next day I related my experience to "Skeets" and the rest of the coaches. We were all anxious to get into the gym at 3:00 and watch him work out with the rest of the players. He walked from the dressing room, a sight to behold. He was wearing a gray T-shirt so short that a good three inches of his pot belly hung out over his knee-length cut-off levi's. His gym shoes were black, his socks heavy gray wool hunting socks with the red and green stripes folded over just under the knee. I silently hoped he could play better than he looked.

A five-on-five pickup game soon got underway. It was quickly apparent that he was not kidding about being able to "do it" with the basketball. He was an uncanny dribbler and passer. Then came his first shot. Sure enough, a "thirty foot springer." SWISH, it went in, as he called out in glee "BUNNY" and took a quick peek at the coaches to see if we were looking. "This guy can't be real," I mumbled as I shook my head. Next time down the floor, "BUNNY" he called again as he launched another thirty foot springer that hit nothing but the bottom of the net. For the next thirty minutes, "Magic" put on an exhibition that I have not seen the likes of since.

"We might have the best guard in America," I exclaimed to "Skeets" as we joyfully strode from the gym.

His incredible shooting exhibition was short-lived, however. He must have used up all his successful "thirty foot springers" in that one afternoon, since during the next two years he struggled with his field goal accuracy. He was a great asset to our club, however, with his ball handling, team leadership, and enthusiastic, gregarious personality. To this day, "Magic" has a special warm spot in my heart.

It has been my experience that junior college players usually fall into one of three categories. First, there are those outstanding players who do not have good enough grades to be admitted to a major college. Second are the outstanding players who have had so many problems with citizenship that major college coaches simply do not want to recruit. Third, there are the late developers who are not physically ready for major college competition upon graduation from high school.

At Clark College we had an assortment of players who fell into each of these three categories. One player that we will refer to as Bob was the son of a minister. He was a local high school product with the reputation of being a great shooter. His game stopped there, however, in that he was a very selfish, non-team oriented person. Unfortunately, his opinion of himself and his basketball ability was overinflated. As the year progressed, he became a constant irritant to our team unity. I was constantly having to discipline him for one problem after another.

Another player we recruited from Portland, Oregon, was Matt Jones. Matt was a fine young man and a fairly talented player, but he was not blessed with great academic skills and did not have sufficient grades to pursue a normal college curriculum. Matt studied welding and mechanical arts at Clark, and today he is earning a fine living working at the Portland shipyards as a welder.

One day during practice, Bob got upset at Matt and called him a "stupid nigger". Matt, who stood 6 ft 4 in and weighed a rock-hard 195 pounds, was normally a very low-key, easy-going guy. But when Bob accosted him verbally, Matt saw red and charged after Bob like a bull chasing a flag. Like the coward he was, Bob ran away with Matt chasing him all over the gym. I knew if Matt caught him it would probably be a violent, one-sided, bloody scene. I chased after Matt, while my assistant Denny Huston tried to intercept Bob. When I caught up with him, I jumped on his shoulders in an attempt to stop him. Matt was so strong and so angry that he simply continued on his chase, dragging me along behind him like a rag doll.

We finally got them both under control, and I took them into my office to see if we could straighten things out. It was obvious that Bob had no remorse and that we had a serious problem on our hands. I asked Matt to get dressed and go home so that I could visit with Bob alone. After a lengthy one hour session with Bob, I was further convinced that we had a cancer in our program that had to be eliminated. Therefore, I instructed Bob to turn in his equipment. I was cutting him from the squad. For the first time since I had known him, Bob showed some humble emotion. He bawled like a baby and pleaded with me to reconsider. Had it just been the single incident of that day, I would have done so, but it was an accumulation of weeks of one disciplinary act after another that prompted me to take such action.

Later that evening Bob's father showed up at my house. For the first hour we politely discussed his son's conduct and my concerns about keeping him on the squad. He asked me to reconsider, but I stood firm in my decision. It was then that I recognized a good portion of the source of Bob's unstable personality. His father's ministerial demeanor quickly changed. A few of his choice comments at that time made it easy for me to see that Bob was simply a "chip off the old block."

Despite the conglomeration of personalities and problems unique only to JC teams, the two years I coached at Clark proved to be enjoyable as well as successful. Each year we placed second in our conference and went to the Washington State JC Tournament.

During the spring of 1976, following the state tournament, I discovered a fool-proof way to lose weight: Fifteen pounds worth in less than two months. Several of the coaches and other faculty members entered a team in the intramural slow pitch softball league. The members of our basketball squad got together and also entered a team. One Thursday afternoon we were scheduled to play each other. I normally played shortstop, but against the basketball team we decided that I should play left field. Our sports information director, Bob Mosier, was to play center. Bob was a former Oklahoma State University basketball player. Frankly, I think he played less than I did at Idaho State.

Dan Duerwader, one of our better athletes hit a long fly ball between Bob and I. We both started after it. It quickly became apparent to me that I could make a fairly easy running catch, so I called out "I've got it, I've got it!" As I reached up with my gloved hand to make the catch, I was greeted with a sudden and extremely painful "WHACK" right on the point of my chin. I was hit by Bob's shoulder as he was running at full stride. He later confessed to me that although he heard me call for the ball, he figured he could slip in front of me and make a spectacular catch. You would have to know Bob Mosier well to appreciate the humor of that statement. He was the brunt of many a joke at Clark College for his frustrated athletic career.

At any rate, I actually saw stars as I fell to the ground in a painful, bloody heap. There was no doubt in my mind that my jaw had been fractured. My four front lower teeth were a good 1 — 1 1/2 inches down my throat, still attached to the mandible (jaw bone). Everyone quickly gathered around me and began to argue about whether to take me to a dentist or a doctor. After what seemed like an eternity, I spit out a mouthful of blood and suggested very strongly that somebody get a car and get me to the hospital quickly.

I buried my face in a towel, was helped into a car, and started the twenty-minute drive to the Kaiser Permanente Hospital in Portland. We arrived about 1 p.m. They rushed me to the emergency ward, where I proceeded to sit and wait in a wheelchair for the next thirty minutes until they could get around to X-raying my jaw. After another thirty minutes of very painful movement for X-rays and their development, a doctor came to me and said, "You have a broken jaw." I thought to myself, "You've got to be kidding—I knew that two hours ago. When the devil is somebody going to do something to stop the pain?" My anguish was just beginning, however.

The hospital was very crowded, so they put me in a bed and wheeled it to the corner of a hallway on the surgical floor to await a room vacancy. I sat there with my face in a towel for the next four hours. When my wife walked in at six o'clock I was seething with anger as well as pain. She had been away from the house, and nobody had been able to locate her until after 5 p.m. When she walked up to me she was the first person to visit me since I had been placed in that bed. I couldn't talk, so I motioned to her to get me a pencil and paper. She did, whereupon I wrote, "Will someone please get me a damn doctor!" When Bee realized that I had not been attended to since the X-rays, she was more angry than I. She stormed away from my bed, and within minutes a doctor was by my side. I don't know what she said, but I've since considered having her make a few comments to some referees for me!

The doctor shot me with a painkiller, took some fine piano wire, wrapped it around the teeth which were still lodged down my throat, and with the aid of some pliers pulled them back up to their normal placement. The next morning I had surgery to repair this displacement, plus one other fracture where the mandible hinges with the skull near the ear. They wired my teeth together, not only left and right, but the upper jaw to the lower jaw as well. For the next two months I could eat nothing but liquids and strained foods. It was rather depressing to be a grown man eating Gerber's baby food three times a day, though a great way to lose weight.

When the job opportunity at Clark College first became a possibility, I talked to Steve Belko at Oregon to get his impression. He suggested strongly that I accept the position, if for no other reason than it would get me back into the Pacific northwest. If an opening were to occur at the University of Oregon, I would, therefore, have a better chance of being hired.

It was no secret that for the two years I coached at Clark I was hoping for something to materialize at the U of O. One day in April of 1966, I received a call from Belko. "Are you alone?" he asked. "Oh boy," I thought to myself, "He must want to talk to me about the job." I closed the door to my office and assured him I was.

"We're interested in a player from Gray's Harbor JC," he stated. "I'm hoping you will be able to give me some information about him." I was crushed. No job—he just wanted info.

Two weeks later I got another call from Steve. Same question: "Alone?" Once again my heart skipped a beat. "Maybe this time he's calling about the job." No such luck, though. He simply needed to know about another prospect.

A month passed and I received yet another call from him. He asked the usual question, "Are you alone?" Skeets was in the office, but I had been disappointed twice before, so this time I answered affirmatively, even though it would not be a private conversation. "No big deal," I thought, "we can certainly discuss recruits even though

Skeets is listening."

"Frank, I've just received authorization to hire a full-time assistant coach; are you still interested?" I tried to remain calm and poised as I assured him I was. Inwardly I was as excited as a cat in a thunderstorm.

I drove to Eugene the next day to discuss the job with him, and within the week I signed a contract to be Steve's first full-time assistant at the U of O.

The 1964 Pocatello High School Indians.

5

FULL TIME IN THE BIG TIME

The year that I had spent at the University of Oregon as a graduate assistant during 1962-63 helped make the transition to the new position quite comfortable. The next five years were to be some of the most enjoyable and rewarding, as well as some of the most traumatic years of my professional career.

Because Coach Belko had been put into the virtually impossible situation of coaching major college basketball with no full-time assistant, the program had fallen on lean years. My new responsibilities were two-fold. First, I was to recruit basketball players for the U of O that could compete successfully with the other major powers on the west coast. Second, I was to act as the academic coordinator for all of our players. In other words, I had to oversee their academic pursuits to make sure that they were registered for such classes that would not only maintain their eligibility, but lead them towards graduation as well. Both responsibilities were full-time challenges. (Most major universities have separate assistant coaches in charge of each area.) Nevertheless, as demanding as they were on my time, I was grateful then and evermore grateful now for the experience I gained while "learning the ropes."

When we arrived at Oregon in 1966, the average crowd was approximately three or four thousand per game. In all the years that Steve Belko had been the head basketball coach at the University of Oregon, he had never had a full-time assistant coach. Rather, he had two half-time coaches. Don Kirsch, the head baseball coach, helped him the first half of the season until baseball practices began; and then he left. Phil McHugh was an assistant football coach who picked up the basketball assistant chores after football finished. It was virtually an impossible situation for Belko to run a first-level major college program with this handicap. Both Don and Phil were very capable basketball men, but they simply could not recruit effectively under these conditions.

Steve Belko confers with Phil McHugh as Don Kirsch listens.

During my first year at the University of Oregon, I noticed, during the first few games, a group of young businessmen who always sat together under the basket in the bleachers. With only three or four thousand fans per game, people could sit virtually anywhere they chose in the 10,500 seat McArthur Court. This particular group caught my eye because of their extremely enthusiastic support for our beleaguered team (last place), their constant harrassing of the officials, and their overall zest for the game. As I became acquainted with these men, I found that they all had season tickets in the premium chair seats; but they relegated their wives to those seats while they congregated together to "raise cane" under the basket.

I affectionately dubbed them the "Under-the-Basket Gang." Some of them worked together at the Harris-Upham Stock Brokerage Exchange in Eugene. Their manager was Myron Bagley. The others included Tony Keller, whose wife was our basketball secretary; Bob Kraus; Gus Keller, who managed the John Warren Hardware Store; Charlie Warren, the owner's son and a former University of Oregon great; Peter Murphy, a Notre Dame graduate who was part owner in the Murphy Logging Corporation; Joe Gonyea, who owned a small lumber business; Jack Boetcher, a banker; Bob Glass, a dentist; and a few more whom I certainly remember by face, but I am embarrassed to say I can't recall their names. Together we organized a recruiting network that resulted in the signing of nine outstanding freshmen and junior college transfers the first year of our recruiting efforts.

1966 at the University of Oregon

A noticeable change began to take place with our crowds. During the second season (the freshman year for the recruits), we would often have six or seven thousand fans in attendance at our frosh preliminary games. The frosh team was a very talented, exciting group of players to watch. We hired a good friend of mine and a very successful coach from West High School in Salt Lake City to coach them. Steve Heiner was his name, and he did an outstanding job. Their record for the year was 19-1 with the one loss chalked up while a couple of the stars were not playing because of a disciplinary matter.

On the other hand, the varsity was still struggling with less talented, although older, more experienced players. As irony would have it, two or three thousand fans would leave after the frosh game, leaving only the usual small number of fans for the varsity games once again.

By the time the frosh players became sophomores and were eligible for varsity competition, the scene at McArthur Court was making a dramatic change. The "Under-the-Basket Gang" could no longer sit in their hallowed seats because the students began to come in force, and the bleacher seats under the basket belonged to them. The gang, therefore, were forced to sit with their wives in their regular reserved seats.

Our average crowd attendance vastly improved as did our win-loss record. We averaged nearly eight or nine thousand fans per game, with a few sellouts.

The initial varsity team I worked with during the 1966-67 season was not blessed with a great deal of size, let alone talent. Our center was a fine young man and certainly an adequate player named John Pinkstaff. John was only 6 ft 7 in, however. He was a fine outside shooter and really should have been playing at the forward position. He was our tallest player, though, and was stuck at center. We had a legitimate major college guard named Nick Jones. Nick was 6 ft 2 in, extremely quick and could play with the best of them. Our other three starters were a 5 ft ll in guard, a 6 ft 5 in and 6 ft 6 in forwards. All three were adequate players, but collectively we were simply not a contending team.

We were scheduled to play the national champions, UCLA, coached by the legendary John Wooden, one of the finest gentlemen and greatest coaches the game has ever known, at Eugene in February 1967. Lew Alcindor was in his sophomore year. They were a far superior team. Coach Belko devised a game plan that I found to be one of the most interesting I have personally been involved with. If we could execute it successfully, he felt we would have a legitimate chance to upset the Bruins. If we were to play them heads up, we would more than likely be blown out.

Our game plan was as follows. As long as we were within six points of UCLA, we would run our special offense. Once they took a 7-point or greater lead we would attempt to play our normal game against them.

When the game started, Alcindor controlled the tip and UCLA subsequently scored. It was 2-0. We went directly to our special offense. Nick Jones was being defended by Mike Sweek. We felt Nick was the better of the two players. John Pinkstaff was positioned at the high post. We knew that Alcindor would stay in the keyhole near the basket to pick up any drives. Our other three players were stationed in a cluster on the free-throw line extended on the right side of the court. Nick was instructed to drive one-on-one against Sweek on the left side as far as he could go. John was then to loop around behind Nick for a pass, assuming that Alcindor would stay under the basket to stop Nick's penetration. Our other three players were not to move, except for an occasional release pass.

If Nick could drive and take a quick 10—15 foot jump shot, he would do so. If not, he would drive and pitch it back to John, who would normally have a 15—18 foot jump shot. We would give up the offensive rebound to Alcindor if we missed (he would get it 95 percent of the time anyway), and our other three players would rush back to stop the UCLA fast break. If neither Nick nor John had a shot, we would get it back to Nick, re-position everyone and try the same attack again.

Steve and I watch intently as Nick drives toward Alcindor.

That was the total offense, repeated over and over again until we got a good shot. It was not intended to be a delay game, but as it worked out the half-time score ended up being 20-16 in favor of UCLA. We felt good about being so close.

Coach Wooden had a surprise for us the second half. He had instructed his Bruins to control the tip and go into a delay game. He later explained to me that while he would never stall at home, he would on the road against an opponent who attempted to stall against his team first. It was his way of expressing dissatisfaction with the stall game and perhaps "feed the fire" for the thirty second clock.

At any rate, we were pleased to see the stall. We felt it enhanced our chances of staying close until the final minutes of the game. We further felt that if the game were close near the end, anyone had a chance to win.

With about three minutes to play, UCLA still maintained about a six-point lead. Few fouls had been called. At that juncture we started gambling in an effort to steal the ball or foul if we were unsuccessful. After the sixth team foul we fouled Alcindor exclusively in an effort to get him off the boards and on the line. He was not a great free-throw shooter, so we hoped to trade them either a field goal for a missed free throw, maybe two for one (point) or at worse two for two.

Well, it was an interesting game plan, and a very tense and dramatic game; but when the wash was hung out to dry, the final score was UCLA 34, UO 25. It had been worth the try.

Our traditional rival was, of course, Oregon State University. There are many great rivalries in America, and the UO-OSU series is one of the best.

One year we were playing them at Corvallis, when Slats Gill was still coaching, and Mel Counts was the Beaver 7 foot center. We didn't feel we could contain him, so Coach Belko instructed our players to use a 2-3 zone when Counts was in the game, but to change to a M/M defense when he went out. Coach Gill substituted quite frequently for Counts, so the game plan would allow us to change defense often.

When the game started, one of our players was confused and instead of playing a zone, he was playing Terry Baker M/M. I mentioned the screw-up to Belko, but he said it looked pretty effective and to let it go. About four minutes into the game, Coach Gill took Counts out. Our team, therefore, switched to a M/M defense: all except our one player who promptly started zoning the guard line. By now, Gill and all the Beavers were really confused as to what kind of defense we were running. Slats called a time-out to regroup. In the huddle our player confessed that he had made a mistake and would, therefore, get together with the rest of the team. "Oh, no you won't," cried Belko. "It's great. You just keep doing what you've been doing." Before OSU could figure our "custom defense," we had a respectable lead and went on to upset them 54-50. That is what is called "coaching flexibility."

Another example of coaching flexibility took place in a game against Northwestern in the Far West Classic in December 1964. I was still at Clark College but helping scout for the Ducks during the classic. Northwestern had a center who was a potential All-American. He was playing on a badly injured leg, however. It was heavily taped from the ankle to the groin. Nevertheless, he was putting on a one-man clinic against us. He was going around us, through us, and over us, scoring at will.

We were in a M/M defense. As a matter of fact, UO had not used anything but a M/M defense for the past year and a half. Coach Belko did not like to use a zone defense except in extreme situations. He had not even worked on a zone defense the entire year.

Furious with the way things were going against Northwestern, Belko called for a time-out. The players quickly gathered around him at the bench. "ZONE 'EM," he demanded.

The players looked at each other in bewilderment. "B..B...But Coach, we don't even..." noticing the fire in his eyes they continued, "...what kind of a zone do..."

"DON'T ASK ANY STUPID QUESTIONS—JUST ZONE 'EM!!!"

When time-in was called I had never seen such a group of hustlin', scrappin', unorganized togetherness swarming all over the poor Northwestern center. In a matter of minutes we regained the lead and went on to win 82-74.

I learned a lesson from that experience. Intensity, togetherness, and determination can often be far more effective than exotic, technical strategies.

The first recruiting year at the U of O resulted in the signing of eight high school graduates and one junior college transfer. Several of the players attended Lane Community College during the summer, prior to their enrollment at Oregon. Therefore, we had to line up part-time jobs for those who lived in Eugene that summer. Transportation was a problem, so four or five of the guys went together, threw in $20 each, and bought an old '41 Chevrolet clunker to get them around town. It wasn't much, but it had four wheels and an engine.

One of the players was a graduate of Gardena High School in Los Angeles, Carlton Slater. Carlton was the runner-up for the Most Valuable Player of L.A. City Schools his senior year. (Curtis Rowe of UCLA was the MVP.) To this day there are some great stories floating around Eugene about Carlton and his exploits while a student-athlete at Oregon.

We got Carlton a part-time job as a fire watch for the Murphy Logging Corp. He was responsible for being at the logging site for four hours after operations had shut down to check equipment and watch for undetected potential fire hazards. His particular site was located sixteen miles from Eugene up the McKenzie River Pass. He reported at 4:00 p.m. each afternoon. To get to the logging site, Carlton had to drive their clunker sixteen miles up the highway and then an additional mile up a very steep one-lane logging truck road to the top of a small mountain where the timber was being cut. It was a great job for a young man raised in the metropolis of Los Angeles.

One hot summer evening in late July I got a phone call just after 8 p.m. It was Carlton. "Coach, I got a big problem."

"What can I help you with Carlton?"

"I jest got in a wreck."

"You what?"

"I jest got in a wreck. I ran our car into a ditch."

"Are you hurt?"

"No—I'm O.K. I got a cut on my leg, but the red corpuscles are taking over the white corpuscles, so I'm O.K." (Carlton was taking a class in first aid at Lane CC and was impressing me with his new knowledge of healing powers.)

"How did the wreck happen?"

"I was driving down that steep logging road after work. I put the car in low gear so I wouldn't go too fast, and I heard this "PING". I guess the transmission or sumpthin' busted 'cause I started goin' faster. I musta been goin' about 40 miles per hour, so I stepped on the brakes and I heard another "PING" and my brakes busted too. By now I was goin' at least 60 mph, so I turned off my key like they taught me in drivers training and drove into the ditch. I was scared, so I jest got my boots and my Bible and got outa there quick. The car's still in the ditch, can you come and get me?"

"Where are you now?"

"I'm calling from the farm house at the bottom of the loggin' road jest off the highway."

"Sit tight, I'll be there in thirty minutes."

I called Steve Belko to report what had happened. He told me to drop by his house and pick him up. His wife was trying to get him to go to a birthday party for "some old fogie" and this would give him a good excuse to get out of it.

On our way up the pass we discussed Carlton's phone call some more. As serious as it was, we couldn't help but laugh at the way Carlton explained his dilemma. Red corpuscles....white corpuscles...PING....40 mph....60 mph...turn off the key...ditch it...boots and Bible and get out. By the time we arrived at the farm house, we were in stitches.

Carlton was sitting on the front steps with the lady of the house. When he saw us, he hurried to our car favoring a slight limp. We supressed our smiles. "You sure you're O.K., Carlton?"

"Yeah, thanks Coach, I'm jest fine now."

"Where's the car?"

"It's just around the corner—whanna see it?"

"Sure, maybe we can get it started and see what's wrong with it."

"Oh, I don't think so, Coach."

We walked around a clump of trees and started down the logging road. About 100 yards ahead of us we could see the road take a sharp 90 degree turn and head up the small mountain. It was much longer and steeper than I had envisioned. But we couldn't see the car.

"Where's the car, Carlton?"

"It's up here in the ditch, Coach. Come on, I'll show ya."

When we got closer to the sharp turn in the road, what Belko and I had envisioned as a car in the ditch off the side of the road suddenly took on a new and very different dimension. There was no ditch running alongside of the mountain road. As the road made the sharp bend toward the farm house, the landscape elevated much like the end of a ski jump. Beyond the mound of dirt was an enormous swampy area filled with two feet of water. This was Carlton's "ditch." The car had obviously not been able to negotiate the curve it was going so fast. Instead, it went straight ahead, off the "ski jump", flew at least thirty feet in the air, hit nose first in the "ditch" leaving a crater in the mud about four feet deep and then flipped over, landing upside down in the swamp water. It was then that Carlton got his "boots and Bible and got outa there quick."

Belko and I looked at the car and then at each other. Our faces were ashen white. It was no longer funny. I must admit, however, that since that day we have had many more good laughs about the incident.

When questioned later about how he escaped injury, Carlton

further explained that when the car took off and went airborne he simply wrapped his arms and legs around the steering wheel like a monkey and "rode it out." Since he was only 5 ft 9 in, I guess he could probably do just that.

The players sold the car sight unseen to a junk dealer for $25.

The junior college player we recruited that first year was Billy Gaskins from Washington D.C. Billy, a 6 ft 2 in guard was selected the player of the year in the nation's capital his senior year.

Steve Belko.   Billy Gaskins and Stan
                                Love.

Billy and Carlton were both involved in a rather unique exhibition of "how to break the press" in a ball game against Florida State.

Our new recruits were now sophomores (including Carlton) and Billy was a senior. We were playing Hugh Durham's Florida State Seminoles at Tallahassee in December 1969. Dave Cowens was a senior for the Seminoles.

The first half FSU put a full court 1-2-1-1 zone press on us with Cowens playing tight on the man with a ball out of bounds. We were having an extremely difficult time getting the ball in bounds, let alone up the court. At half time we were down 20 points.

We obviously needed to make some adjustments. Carlton was not a starter, but he was an exceptional dribbler and passer. After some deliberations we decided to start Carlton and Billy as guards the second half and attempt a new way of getting the ball inbounds against the press. Belko explained the strategy:

"Billy, when Florida State scores you take the ball out of bounds on the right side of the basket. Cowens will be all over you with the press. Carlton, as soon as Billy gets out of bounds on the right side, you jump out of bounds on the left side about 20 feet from Billy. Billy will pass the ball to you, still out-of-bounds. You can then in-bounds the ball without Cowens harrassing you. Do you understand?"

"Got cha Coach," they both assured him.

The second half started. Florida State controlled the tip, promptly scored, and initiated the 1-2-1-1 press once again. As per our halftime discussion, Billy took the ball out of bounds on the right side and Carlton jumped out of bounds on the left side. Cowens was all over Billy as we anticipated. Unfortunately, Billy got flustered and when he passed the ball across to Carlton he threw it over his head. It went three to four rows up into the stands. The seats were the telescopic foldout bleacher type with no backs. In his excitement, Carlton chased the ball right up into the fourth row, knocking down people, popcorn flying every which way. He quickly retrieved the ball, looked up—and guess what he saw. Here comes Cowens right into the stands after him. Carlton stood on his tip toes on row four and passed down court to an open man. The five seconds had easily expired, but the ref stood in dumbfounded amazement and let the play progress.

On the pass, Carlton almost hit Belko in the head, who had stood up to see what was happening with Carlton up in the stands. "TIME OUT," Belko embarrassingly requested as he ducked.

"Settle down now fellas, we'll be O.K. The strategy will work if we will just make good passes. Tell you what. This time Carlton you take the ball out on the left side and pass it to Billy who's a little bigger on the right side. Make a good pass now. Let's go!"

After FSU's next basket, Carlton quickly took it out as Belko had instructed. Cowens pressed him. Billy jumped out-of-bounds and Carlton made a perfect pass to him. So far so good. Billy looked up and couldn't find an open man. So he did the next best thing. He dribbled the ball inbounds and up the court. Cowens looked at the ref, the ref looked at Carlton, Carlton looked at Billy, cupped his mouth with his hands and hollered, "Come back Billy, you-all can't do that." FSU won 100-84.

The five years we spent at the University of Oregon were very enjoyable and rewarding years. The 1968-69 season, however, was marred by an incident that has been far and above the most distasteful and traumatic experience I have gone through in my professional career.

It was the era when the Viet-Nam War was causing much campus unrest, and the hippie movement was beginning to take hold. Athletes across the country were expressing their "individuality" by insisting upon wearing long hair, beards and goatees. The Black students and athletes were growing long bushy "Afro" hairdos. Right or wrong, such grooming standards caused great consternation with coaches and fans alike. Many coaches from the "old school" preferred their athletes keeping their hair cut short. The majority of fans and alumni were even more uptight than coaches. Thousands and thousands of dollars that normally were donated to athletic support funds were withdrawn in protest to the liberal relaxation of grooming standards by athletic departments. Most coaches were forced to relax their standards simply because the university administration would not support their conservative views. It rapidly became a nationwide problem.

When the problem first surfaced during the 1967-68 season we had a meeting of the entire athletic department coaching staff to establish a policy. We decided collectively that we would hold to the short haircut and beardless grooming code. We would allow well-groomed mustaches. We further decided that in all fairness to the athletes, we would explain our policy to each young man as we recruited him. Then the choice was his: to join us and accept our policy or choose another university. I am convinced we lost a couple of outstanding basketball players that spring because of our policy.

School commenced, and we went throughout the fall and into the winter without incident. We had played Utah and North Carolina on the road to open our basketball season. After the North Carolina series, the team returned to Eugene. I flew to New York City to scout Yale in a game played at Fordham in the Bronx. We were to play Yale later that month in the Far West Classic. The next day I returned to Eugene and arrived about 6 p.m. I had previously scheduled an 8 p.m. practice with the freshman team. In addition to being in charge of recruiting and academic coordination, I also coached the freshman team that year. Our first game was to be played the next evening in Portland.

That night at practice two new players joined us for the first time. They were Bobby Moore and Billy Drake from off the football team. Although our basketball squad had been practicing for over one and a half months, football had just finished, so this was their first practice. It was obvious that the football coaches had let the grooming standards slip because both Billy and Bobby were sporting long "Afro" hairstyles. Some of the regular basketball players were also getting rather shaggy and in need of a haircut.

At the conclusion of practice, I called the twelve players together and discussed our code of conduct for road trips. I told Bobby and Bill that even though they had only been to one practice, we would be pleased to take them on this first trip. I then reviewed with the entire team our athletic department grooming code. I explained to Bobby, Bill, Ken Strand and a couple of other players that they would have to get their hair trimmed to a moderate length if they wanted to make the trip.

After the meeting, Bobby and Bill came to me and explained their concern about getting haircuts. "How short do we have to cut it?" they inquired. I explained that I didn't expect them to get "scalped," but it needed to be trimmed somewhat. I suggested that the length it was when they started school in the fall would be appropriate. That seemed to satisfy them, and they took off.

The next morning I was in the restroom near my office at MacArthur Court when Coach Belko came in sort of snickering and informed me that there were a half dozen guys in our athletic department offices wanting to see me. "Looks like they're kinda mad," he chuckled. My curiosity was whet as I walked to Athletic Director Len Casanova's office to see what was up. When I arrived, I was greeted by six older Black students who were staring daggers right through me. "Sit down, Frank," Director Casanova instructed. "These men are from the Black Student Union and have lodged a protest that you threatened to leave Bobby Moore and Bill Drake home from the freshman basketball trip if they didn't cut off their 'Afros'." With that, all six of them started in on me simultaneously, cursing me, accusing me of racism, bigotry, attacking my religious beliefs, etc., etc.

"WHOA—WAIT JUST A MINUTE!!!" I insisted. "I'll be darned if I'm going to walk in here and be accosted by six guys off the street whom I don't even know and who obviously don't have the slightest idea what they're talking about." I suggested that they first identify themselves by introducing themselves to me and then calmly explaining their concerns. Once again they started calling me obscene names and jabbering incoherently. I stood up and firmly explained, "Gentlemen, I told you once, and I am going to tell you again: I will not sit here and be accosted by a bunch of jabbering fools. If you want to calm down, introduce yourselves and explain your complaint like civilized human beings, I'll discuss the problem we obviously have. If not—I'm gone!!"

One guy promptly introduced himself defiantly as "Malcolm X". A second as Muhammad A and a third as Eliza Z. With that, I walked out of the office as I exclaimed that they knew the ground rules—come back when they're ready to play the game.

One hour later, Len Casanova called me back into his office. He explained that he had just received a phone call from the President's office and that he wanted me, Casanova and Ron Straton to meet in his office with three members of the Black Student Union at 1 p.m. (Ron was an assistant football coach. He was the only Black coach on the University of Oregon athletic staff at the time. Today, he is an investigator for the NCAA.)

It seemed like a sensible and reasonable way to discuss the apparent problem, so Ron, Cas and I went to the President's office for the 1 p.m. meeting. Actually the U of O did not have a full-time President. He had resigned a few months previously, and while the search committee was seeking a replacement, a U of O professor was appointed as the interim president. Therefore, it was with the interim president that we were to meet with the three BSU leaders.

We arrived a few minutes early and were ushered into the President's office. After a few minutes of small talk, the door to his office burst open and in rushed not three, but 21 members of the Black Student Union. They had forced their way past his secretary and crowded into his office. I thought to myself, "Oh boy, here we go again."

It was obvious from the beginning that the President, who was a very timid man, was sorely lacking in leadership qualities. He was frightened and didn't know how to handle this nasty situation. In an attempt to calm this angry mob, he suggested that we leave his office and adjourn to the conference room which would be big enough to accommodate all 25 people.

Once in the conference room, we seated ourselves around the big conference table. The interim President was a couple of seats to my left, separated from me by Ron and Cas. To his left, around the table, and then to my right were the 21 BSU members.

The interim President proposed that we each stand and express ourselves so that he could get a clear understanding of the dilemma. We would start to his left. One after another, the BSU members would stand and berate me. With but two or three exceptions, they would curse me, call me names, and attack my religious beliefs. For over sixty minutes and 21 speakers I had to sit there and accept their verbal abuse. Not on time did the acting president intercede or attempt to bring the dialogue to some sort of civilized state. On several occasions when the accusations became particularly nasty, I would look at him to see his reaction. For virtually the entire hour he sat motionless, his hands clasped in front of him at the table, his head bowed as he stared into space. It was, without question, the worst hour of my entire life. Never have I seethed with more anger nor contempt than I did at that time: Not only at the people who were attacking me without justification, but at the interim president for allowing it to take place.

When it was my turn to speak, I stood and began to explain the athletic department grooming code and that the demand for haircuts was for every member of our team, not just Bobby and Bill. As I spoke, I was continuously and openly cursed in an effort to shout me down. I had my say, and then Cas and Ron defended my stand.

Everyone had had an opportunity to speak. The acting President then suggested that the original group of three BSU leaders meet with Ron, Cas and me in his office and that the remaining people leave us at that time. Several people objected vehemently, but the BSU leaders finally convinced the rest to leave.

When we adjourned to the President's office we discussed the matter for a few more minutes, and then the interim President made a statement: "Coach Arnold, after listening to all the factors involved, it is my decision that you have no right to require haircuts of the players, and so you will allow them to make the trip to Portland tonight as they are presently groomed."

His ruling did not surprise me. I retaliated: "Mr. President, in all due respect, Sir, you are wrong. You have sat here and listened to a biased militant group and based your decision solely on what you have heard in a one hour period of time. Our athletic department has discussed the problem repeatedly. We have a staff that collectively chose to administer the grooming code, although we do have some members who do not enforce it. The vast majority of our athletes not only accept the code but endorse it. The members of our university, community, both alumni and non-alumni supporters overwhelmingly desire that our athletes remain moderately groomed." And then I dropped the bombshell, "I am sorry, Sir, but I cannot accept your ruling. Without the support of the administration in reasonable disciplinary matters a coach's authority will quickly crumble. If you want these players to go on the trip without adhering to our grooming code then you take them—I will not." I concluded by saying, "Furthermore, Sir, I am appalled and disguested by the way you sat there and let these people treat a fellow human being so obscenely. I strongly feel that you owe me an apology and would hope that after you have a chance to review what has gone on today you will see fit to offer me that apology."

I politely excused myself and left the office. I did not take the team to Portland that night, nor did I coach them for the next five games. I was prepared to resign my position entirely. I have strong beliefs that people must not be hypocritical. If they cannot endorse nor accept something of significance, then they must not be a part of it. A man must have the courage of his convictions, or he is no man at all. At the same time, one must always be willing to listen and learn, and even change if change is for the better.

Within the next week several other distasteful events took place. My wife received a few anonymous but very obscene and threatening letters in the mail. Several dozen obscene pamphlets were dumped on the front door step of the LDS church houses near the campus. All in all, life was pure hell.

I sought the counsel of my stake presidency (a local religious tribunal) in Eugene: Ralph Lake, Bob Hill, and Don Ainge. These were three great men who advised me to be strong in my convictions, yet understanding, fair and honest in my dealings with people of different beliefs.

One night three U of O supporters to whom I was very close visited me at my house. It had been such an unpleasant week that Bee and I were on the verge of handing in my resignation. Myron Bagley, Gus Keller, and Tony Keller would have no part of it. They encouraged me to hang tough and see it through to the end. None of us were really sure what the end was. At any rate, we chose to stay on and see what would transpire.

After our meeting, the interim President had to leave town for two weeks. When he returned he summoned me to his office. He explained that after considerable thought he agreed that he owed me an apology and then offered one. I accepted. It was concluded by Cas and the head coaches that a compromise needed to be considered. We would continue to require moderate haircuts from our white athletes, but would allow longer "Afros" of the Black athletes. The reasoning was that a Black's Afro would not get into his eyes and affect his performance. Furthermore, more and more Black people were growing long Afros as a part of their culture, and so we would simply allow the norm.

It seemed like a double standard to me, because more and more whites were also growing longer hair. Nevertheless, the AD and head coaches adopted the new rule, and it was something I could certainly live with, so I re-joined the staff and took up all of my responsibilities including the coaching of the freshman team.

A footnote of interest. At the end of the school year, the President of the Black Student Union forced his way onto the speaker podium during graduation exercises, took the microphone from this same interim president, and delivered a militant speech. Later that same afternoon, the interim president climbed into his family Volkswagen, drove up the McKenzie River Highway and ran headon into a logging truck, killing him instantly. Many people to this day feel it was a suicidal act.

The remainder of the month was like a nightmare. The members of the Black Student Union, along with a few sympathizers forced their way into the reserved seats (300 strong) directly behind our home team bench. The administration chose not to challenge them. The season ticket holders, therefore, had to find seating in the general admission section. It was traditional at U of O in those days to have both teams on the floor during the Star Spangled Banner. The lights were turned off and a spotlight put on the flag. This particular group would never stand up for the anthem. Rather, they would cause quite a commotion. I was hit on numerous occasions with thrown objects during "the banner." Once the game started they would berate and belittle the coaches and the white players. They would openly tell the Black players to disobey coaches' directions, etc. There was a great deal of pressure on everyone concerned.

On one occasion they had a protest sit-down on the floor prior to a game, made their militant speeches and marched off. When they left, the floor was covered with several raw eggs. The game was delayed for well over an hour to clean the floor.

They continued their wrath towards me personally and instituted a campaign to have me fired. Just prior to the Christmas vacation, Coach Belko sent me on a scouting trip to Moscow, Idaho, to scout the University of Idaho—an upcoming opponent. I was to scout them on Friday, which would allow me to fly back to Eugene for our Saturday home game. I was somewhat concerned about leaving because of the obscene and threatening mail my wife had received earlier. Nevertheless, I left for the one-day assignment. After the Idaho game I was waiting near the press table for the final stats when the head coach of U of I asked to speak to me privately. He explained that Belko and the U of O Athletic Director, Len Casanova, had called and asked him to inform me of their desire to have me stay in Moscow the next night and scout them a second time. It was a highly unusual request, and I sensed something strange. I immediately called Belko to see what was up. He explained that the militant group would announce a bomb plant at the Saturday game if I was on the bench. Since this was the next-to-last home game prior to a three-week Christmas break, our administration felt that they would cool off in that period of time if I were to stay in Moscow. I was quite concerned for the welfare of my family, however, and told Belko I was coming back to Eugene regardless of the bomb scare. He understood my concern, and we agreed that he would send my family to Portland where I could meet them. We did, in fact, meet in Portland, and had a very difficult evening listening to the ball game on the radio. As good fortune would have it, there was no incident at the game. During the Christmas break we played in the Far West Classic in Portland. No incidents occurred.

Our next home game would be against UCLA on regional TV. It seemed to me that things around campus had returned to normal. Tip-off was scheduled for 8:05. Prior to the game, Belko seemed unusually nervous, but then he always exhibited a certain amount of pre-game jitters. The national anthem was played, and the teams met at center court for the tip-off. After the toss, Belko exhausted a big sigh of relief. I asked him, "What in the devil have you been so uptight about?" He replied, "I'll tell you after the game." It seems as if at 5:00, the president of the BSU confronted Belko in his office and told him that if Arnold was on the bench prior to the game, that during the National Anthem the entire student group of 300 would march around the floor in front of the TV cameras and then exit in a protest boycott. Belko simply said that enough was enough and threw him out of his office. It was obvious to me after his explanation of the incident why he was so nervous before the game and relieved when no incident occurred. That virtually ended any serious problems for the remainder of the year.

After a year of such traumatic experiences, anything else I have encountered pertaining to fan reaction has seemed quite minor. Nevertheless, there have been, and probably always will be, many experiences that all coaches go through, both positive and negative.

After that disrupting season things got back to normal, and we got back to the business of building a contending program. Things moved steadily forward. It has often been said by long-time U of O supporters that the greatest week in Oregon basketball occurred one weekend in February 1970. It was the weekend of the series against USC and UCLA. It was to be the real birth of one of the great home crowds in collegiate basketball history.

The Friday night game was against USC and played in front of a packed house. MacArthur Court buzzed with excitement prior to tip-off. The crowd support and enthusiasm grew with every minute of the game. When it was over, we had upset USC 92-83. The crowd went nuts, but it was nothing compared to what we were to witness 22 hours later.

The mighty UCLA was in town. They were undefeated in 56 consecutive games, and defending NCAA champions. The fever pitch at Mac Court picked up where it left off the night before. The teams took the floor for warm-up, and electricity was everywhere. I had chills and goose-bumps over my entire body as I awaited the introductions. I could sense that something special was about to happen.

The buzzer sounded and the teams went to their respective benches for introduction. UCLA was introduced first. Each player was met with a polite applause. And then the announcer said, "And now for the starting line-up for the University of Oregon." AN EXPLOSION!! I have never witnessed before, nor since, such an eruption from a sports crowd. The students, townspeople, the ushers, little boys, old women, everybody up to the rafters were on their feet yelling and stomping and clapping. I glanced down at Coach Wooden: he too was clapping politely as he always does for the opponent, his famous program rolled up and stuck under his armpit. The volume seemed to go higher, one minute, two minutes; I glanced at Coach Wooden again. He had quietly dropped his hands and was no longer applauding. A simple smile coursed his lips, and he looked about the arena—I believe in appreciation for what the home crowd was doing for its team. The volume seemed to increase even more. I was becoming nervous; it seemed to be so long and intense. I glanced at the main scoreboard above the court. It was actually bouncing on its four cables, as the building rocked with the thunderous noise. A thought passed through my mind that it might break away and come crashing to the floor. I looked at the UCLA players. They were shifting nervously. Then I looked at our U of O players. Their jaws were set, their eyes were afire, they were ready to play.

Finally, after at least three to four minutes of this incredible ovation, Coach Belko instructed the announcer to break off the noise and introduce our team. He did, and the teams finally met at center court for the tip-off. We were out of our heads. We jumped on UCLA quickly, led by ten at half time, and beat them by thirteen, 78-65. Absolute pandemonium took place. The team was mobbed on its way to the dressing room. U of O basketball had arrived.

6

THE UCLA YEARS

The relocation from the University of Oregon to UCLA came about through a series of unusual events. I had just concluded my fifth season as an assistant to Coach Belko. He had pretty well decided to retire, and I was obviously interested in the possibility of becoming the head coach at Oregon.

One morning in April of 1971, a "heavyweight" administrator at the U of O asked me to meet him at a secluded off-campus restaurant. He had something of great importance that he wanted to discuss with me. We met at noon, whereupon he informed me that Steve Belko had confided in him that he was definitely going to retire. In a couple of weeks, Steve was going to Honolulu to coach the West All-Star team in the College All-Star Classic held in Hawaii each spring. Upon his return, he was to hand in his official letter of resignation. Steve was supporting me for the job, and the purpose of the meeting was to establish a "game plan."

The administration asked me if I would be willing to accept the job on a one-year interim basis. I felt insulted. "Why a one-year interim basis?" I inquired.

"Hear me out," he insisted. "We have two problems of concern. First, the confrontations you got caught up with the Black community three years ago could cause some loss of support. It no longer seems to be a problem, but I'm sure there are still a few militants that will stir things up. Second, the football staff has hired nothing but former University of Oregon players and personnel for the last several years. There are some very influential alumni in Portland who are deeply concerned about this inbreeding. That problem could carry over to your situation as well. At any rate, we could eliminate both potential problems if we did this. We will have Steve hold his letter of resignation until just before school starts. When he turns it in, we will simply appoint you as the interim coach on the basis that it would be too late to open the job for other candidates. I have the utmost confidence that after you have had the reigns for a full year you will prove to everyone that it was a wise choice, and then we could hire you full time."

It appeared to be a fool-proof plan, but my pride was too great, and I wanted nothing to do with such an arrangement.

"What do you suggest we do then?" the administrator asked.

"You must open the job up for all comers after Steve resigns, and I will throw my hat in the ring. If I come out on top, I deserve the job, and if I don't, then that too will be in the best interest of the university."

After some deliberation, the administration suggested a compromise. "Tell you what. I will hand-pick and invite four candidates to visit the campus and interview them personally. If one of the four looks like a highly qualified replacement, we will hire him. If none of the four are satisfactory, the head job is yours."

It sounded like a fair and equitable way to handle matters, so I expressed my agreement.

Steve left for Honolulu to coach the All-Star team on a Sunday. On Monday, the administration called and asked if I would mind meeting with the first of the four candidates. I was surprised that they were bringing someone to campus prior to Steve's official resignation but nevertheless agreed to meet with him. It was Dick Harter, the head coach of the University of Pennsylvania. His team had just concluded super back-to-back seasons, and finished the year ranked second in the nation.

Harter was brought to town under the guise of being a candidate of the gymnastics coaching position, which was also open. I met with him secretly at the Thunderbird Inn Restaurant. He asked me several questions about the program, the players and the recruiting. After our discussion, he thanked me and then said that if he got the job there would not be a position available for me, because he had two assistants at Penn that he intended to bring with him. I assured him that I understood such coaching changes, but not to count his chickens before they hatched. I told him that I, too, was a candidate, and thought my base of support was very strong. We parted amiably.

The job was offered to Harter that evening. I received a phone call at 8 p.m. informing me that he had been hired. I was flabbergasted at the speed with which it all happened. The biggest shock was the realization that I was out of a job, that Bee and I and our family of four children no longer had job security. It was a very uneasy, restless evening.

Early the next morning I was in the office of our athletic director, Norv Ritchey. I expressed my consternation about being "out in the street" overnight.

"What do you mean out in the street?" Norv asked.

I explained to him the conversation I had had with Harter regarding assistants the day before. Norv laughed and replied that they had made it perfectly clear to Harter that I was to remain as an assistant basketball coach. It's hard to explain the relief that statement brought to me.

The irony was that Steve had existed for several years without full-time assistants, and five years with only one. Harter not only had to keep me as a full-time assistant, but was allowed to bring his two assistants from Penn as well. Instead of one, he had three assistants.

I thanked Norv for the gesture and assured him I appreciated the security. Nevertheless, I could easily see the writing on the wall. Within a few months I felt certain that I would be relegated to the end of the bench and given menial coaching tasks to perform. I was not interested in such an arrangement and served notice that I would seek a coaching position elsewhere as soon as possible.

This brings us to the UCLA scene. Wednesday afternoon I received a long-distance phone call from Los Angeles. It was Coach John Wooden. He inquired about the rumors pertaining to Steve's stepping down. I explained to him that Steve was about to resign and that Harter would be named as the new head coach. He asked where that left me, and I further explained my status and feelings. Coach Wooden then informed me that his assistant, Denny Crum, had just accepted the head coaching job at the University of Louisville. If I was interested in the position, he would like to talk to me about it.

I had been recruiting the Southern California area for the past five years. Each time I made a trip to Los Angeles I had told myself that there was no way anyone could get me to live in that jungle. When Coach Wooden extended the invitation to discuss the UCLA assistantship with him, it took me all of two seconds to reconsider my feelings about L.A.

I assured him I was extremely interested. As good fortune would have it, I had already scheduled a trip to L.A. the very next day to finalize the organization of an "Orange County Duck Club" that I had been working on for the past year. On Friday I was also to meet with Harter, who was flying from Pennsylvania to L.A. for a press conference and spend three days introducing him and one of his assistants Dick Stewart to the Southern California prospects I had been recruiting.

Coach Wooden wanted to keep our meeting absolutely confidential. He planned to pick me up at the Los Angeles International Airport upon my arrival. From there we would go to a private place to visit. I told absolutely no one about the call except Bee. She was as excited as I was.

I boarded the plane Thursday morning, and much to my chagrin ran into two of our U of O players, Stan Love and Larry Holliday. They both lived in L.A. and were on their way home to visit their folks. I certainly didn't want to have them see Wooden meet me at the airport. We had a thirty minute layover in San Francisco, so I jumped off the plane and called Coach Wooden to report the dilemma. Under the circumstances, he felt it best for me to meet him at his office instead.

I arrived there at 1:30 p.m. trying to hide my nervous anxiety. I wanted that job very badly. In his warm, gentlemanly way, Coach Wooden soon put me at ease. We spent the first half hour talking about me and my family. Soon we were discussing his philosophy of basketball and what the job would entail. He stated that he did not believe in having a first and a second assistant coach. Rather, he wanted co-assistant coaches with different responsibilities. Gary Cunningham, one of the finest people I have ever had the pleasure of knowing, had been with him as a player and as an assistant for ten years. He would work with Coach Wooden with the varsity and handle the academic coordination. If I got the job, I would coach the junior varsity team, scout the opponents, and be in charge of the recruiting. It pleased me when he talked about co-assistant coaches, but in all honesty it really didn't work out that way. For all intents and purposes, Gary was the first assistant, and I was the second. But it made little difference to me. After a very extensive and encouraging meeting, he suggested that I go with him to meet the athletic director, J.D. Morgan. J.D. was, without question, one of the most dynamic, powerful administrators the world of athletics has ever known. I was anxious to meet him more intimately.

We discussed the job responsibilities more in depth, and then J.D. asked how much money it would take to get me to join them at UCLA. Had I been truthful, I would have said $2. Instead, my mind quickly calculated some interesting figures. I happened to know that the $12,000 per year I earned at the U of O made me the second highest paid assistant in the conference. Surely UCLA would be willing to pay their assistant more than that. "$15,000," I said boldly. J.D. didn't bat an eye. "That certainly is fair," he stated. "In addition, we would provide you with room and board expenses until you can find a house and then pay for your moving expenses to L.A." It was so easy I was mad at myself for not asking for more. My glee was quickly tempered, however, with the realization that I had not yet been offered the job.

As Coach Wooden walked me to the door, he explained that he had made a commitment to one of his former players to interview him for the job. Nevertheless, he assured me that my chances of receiving the offer were extremely good. He then asked where he could reach me Monday morning to let me know for sure. We made arrangements for him to call me at the Sheraton-Universal Hotel at 10 a.m. Monday. The next three days of waiting were to be very agonizing.

I finished my business in Anaheim for the Orange County Duck Club later that evening. Harter, Stewart and I met at the Sheraton West Hotel in Los Angeles at noon on Friday for the press conference that had been scheduled to introduce Harter to the big city media. Exactly one sports writer showed up. I guess that says something about how much interest there is in Southern California for athletic programs outside of the city.

After the press conference, the three of us hit the recruiting trail. It was certainly a new experience for me. I had been recruiting about four prospects in the LA area. In the next couple of days we were to visit each of them in their homes. Whereas I had always been alone on such recruiting trips for the past five years, this time I was accompanied by not only the head coach, but another assistant coach as well. After I introduced Harter and Stewart to the prospect and his parents, I sat back and watched them "operate." It was a well-oiled and finely-tuned presentation. I witnessed as they unloaded their "number one" speech. In each home Harter would begin with some small talk and then launch into his recruiting pitch. At a precise moment, Stewart would break in and take over with some specific comments. Shortly, Harter would take over once again in an obviously prearranged point and so on. It was a very dynamic and impressive presentation.

At one point, Harter would make the comment to the recruit how the U of O program would dedicate itself to beating UCLA and taking the "number one" for themselves. Each time I grimaced to myself as I realized that there was a very strong possibility that I would be at UCLA instead of Oregon competing against these two new coaches.

By Sunday afternoon we had concluded our meetings with the four recruits. Harter decided that we should fly to San Francisco for additional recruiting that night rather than wait for our prearranged Monday afternoon flight. I readily agreed, although inwardly I was in a state of panic because Coach Wooden was to call me Monday morning at the hotel to let me know about the UCLA job.

We arrived in San Francisco by 5:30 p.m., and checked into a hotel by the airport. We had made an appointment for 6 p.m. I excused myself from the room, telling Harter and Stewart that I had to pick something up at the gift shop in the lobby. I hurriedly found the pay phone in the lobby and called Coach Wooden at his home. When he answered, I explained to him our sudden change of plans, and where he could contact me the following day. "No need," he explained. "I'm now prepared to offer you the job under the circumstances we discussed Thursday, if you're still interested." At that very moment, I received a tap on the shoulder. It was Harter. "Here's your coat. We're running a bit late, so we had better hurry," he stated.

In my efforts to keep the UCLA scene confidential, I turned back to the phone and responded, "Coach Harter just arrived, so I have to leave now. Everything is affirmative as far as I'm concerned. I'll call you again tomorrow." Coach Wooden understood as we jointly hung up. As of that moment, I was a Bruin.

I returned to Eugene Monday and called UCLA again. We decided it would be best to make a joint press release at precisely 12 noon Wednesday. The resignation of Belko and hiring of Harter had been botched so badly by press leaks that Bee and I chose not to tell anyone about the new assignment until it was officially released. So far, we were lucky that not a soul in Eugene knew of the change. At 11:55 a.m. Wednesday morning I walked into Norv Ritchey's office and handed him my letter of resignation and explained to him the UCLA situation. Norv had always been a very special person and a close friend. He was happy for me.

There was a big spread that evening in the Eugene "Register Guard," the local paper, about my resignation. In the "L.A. Times," my appointment was announced in the last sentence of the last paragraph in a one column article entitled, "Cunningham New Top Aide for UCLA Basketball." Any inclination I may have had of considering myself some kind of hot shot or something because of the UCLA appointment was tempered in a hurry by that humbling announcement.

Volumes have been written about the life of John Wooden and the UCLA basketball program. It has been my experience that a great deal I have read has been distorted, and the lives of Coach Wooden and many of the ball players have been misrepresented. I would like to share with the readers a few of my personal experiences and

J. D. Morgan presents another trophy to Coach Wooden as Gary Cunningham and I observe.

impressions based on four years of initmate involvement with the most successful collegiate basketball program ever.

I moved into the Bel Aire Sands Hotel for a few weeks while my family stayed in Eugene to sell our house. My impressions of Wooden to date had always been external, having received them from observations of him at clinics, as an opponent coach, from writings and from comments by other people. Within a few weeks of my arrival in L.A., I was to receive one more impression, from a former assistant of his, Jerry Norman.

I called Jerry and requested an opportunity to talk to him over lunch one day about the recruiting process at UCLA. Jerry had been Wooden's assistant for several years and had recruited players such as Gail Goodrich, Keith Erickson, Walt Hazzard, and Lew Alcindor. I had for years considered Jerry to be the premier recruiter in America. Denny Crum had replaced Jerry when he resigned to enter the world of financial management.

At lunch Jerry offered one major suggestion pertaining to recruiting for John Wooden and UCLA that he had employed during his tenure with the Bruins. Coach Wooden had already instructed me that I was not to recruit prospective student-athletes from out of the state of California unless such a prospect contacted us first indicating his interest in UCLA. Wooden felt that there were enough outstanding prospects in California alone to make us a national contender each year, if we recruited them successfully. He saw no need to spend the time and money chasing recruits all over America. All of his assistants were under the same restrictive stipulations, including Jerry Norman.

Jerry explained to me, however, that a great deal of his recruiting efforts were spent attempting to get super out-of-state prospects to write Wooden a letter expressing their interest. He made certain that these prospects understood that unless they made the first move they would never be recruited by UCLA. Coach Wooden, of course, was never to know that a great deal of behind-the-scenes work took place before certain prospects did, in fact, initiate first contact. Jerry further suggested that if I wanted to recruit successfully for UCLA that I take his counsel seriously and do the same thing. I did, and the next four years I, too, spent many hours getting certain prospects to write Coach Wooden a letter. Eventually he would bring the letter to my office and suggest that I follow up and look into the young man's credentials.

In retrospect, there is little doubt in my mind that Coach Wooden's philosophy was a wise one. There are so many talented players in California that a university such as UCLA, that consistently recruited successfully the cream of the crop, would be extremely well off. Complement those players with a few great ones from out-of-state who sincerely wanted to attend that university (as compared to being "talked into it" with pressure tactics) and you have a combination for an annual top ten contender.

Jerry Norman also suggested that I might find Coach Wooden himself to be not only the biggest asset I would have in recruiting for UCLA, but somewhat of a liability as well. His statement was not made in a malicious way. Suffice it to say at this time that I soon found that I had a dilemma on my hands. Coach Wooden would take me in his office and tell me how he wanted me to be a very low key, non-aggressive recruiter. The very next day his boss, our Athletic Director, J. D. Morgan, would call me into his office, pound his fist on the desk, and roar that he wanted me to be the most aggressive, relentless recruiter in the country. Try that one on for size, and try to satisfy both men of their stature at the same time. Somehow, I managed to do it.

The first day of practice on October 15 introduced something new to me: Staff meetings. Coach Wooden had Gary and me in his office each morning at 9 a.m. We would take at least two hours each day to meticulously plan a two-hour practice. Every detail of every drill, technique and strategy was discussed daily. We would also spend a great deal of the time discussing the players themselves, their classes, their personalities, and their problems. I found Wooden to be a very compassionate man with a great deal of care and concern for his players.

In time I discovered a very interesting thing about John Wooden. He had the reputation in the public's eye of being a very kind, warm, considerate, grandfatherly type of man. His reputation was justly deserved, because he did, in fact, exhibit all of those characteristics. Behind closed doors, however, and in the world of competition, I found an additional trait. He was not only a genuine nice guy, but also an absolutely fierce competitor. He would never show it publicly, but he had a tiger in his tank that would scratch and fight for its very life when competing. It was a great lesson for me that a person can be both—a gentleman and a gladiator.

Our staff meetings were always the highlight of my day. That first year in particular I did a lot of sitting and listening. In the beginning, I was very reluctant to offer any suggestions. After all, what could a kid from Pocatello have to offer the greatest basketball coach in the history of the game.

When I did offer my first suggestions, I was devastated. He cut it to ribbons and spit it out. I quickly backed off. In time I found that that was his way of determining just how strongly Gary or I really believed in our suggestions. He used to tell us that it's a lot easier to make suggestions than decisions; and by golly, we had better be prepared to defend ourselves if we had something to offer. After several years as a head coach, I concur with his statement about suggestions versus decisions.

There were times when we would get into pretty good discussions. Gary had been with Coach Wooden for over ten years and had already learned to fight for his beliefs. In time, I did as well; and after some very lively discussions, on occasion, Coach would make important and wise decisions that often embraced his assistants' suggestions.

The many hours the three of us spent in his office are absolutely invaluable to me. They were equally as valuable as the practice and games themselves. Nowhere can one read a book or sit in on lectures and benefit as greatly as Gary and I did from actually being in Coach

Wooden's presence daily and absorbing his words of wisdom.

I have often been asked what one thing was the most valuable that I learned from Coach Wooden. There are, of course, many; but I can best answer that question by relating a story that took place during the very first staff meeting we had. It was October 15, 1971.

Coach Wooden gave Gary and me three or four ditto copies of information pertaining to his practice policies, philosophy, etc. One sheet was entitled, "How to Handle Players." The word "Handle", however, had been crossed out and above it the words "Work With" were written instead. Therefore, it read "How to ~~Handle~~ Work With Basketball Players." I thought the change rather interesting, so I inquired as to why it had been made. He told me the story.

Wilt Chamberlain had just been traded to the Los Angeles Lakers. At that time, he had the reputation of a malcontent and had often been accused of getting several coaches fired because they couldn't get along. Butch Van Breda Koff had also been recently hired as the new coach for the Lakers, and Butch was a very aggressive, fiery-type coach.

When Wilt flew to Los Angeles, a press conference was held at the L.A. International Airport upon his arrival. Coincidentally, Coach Wooden happened to be at the same terminal gate when the press conference got underway. During the interview, one sportscaster asked Wilt, "Can Van Breda Koff handle you?" Wilt calmly replied, "Nobody can *handle* me. You *handle* animals. Anybody can *work with* me."

That so impressed Coach Wooden that when he returned to his office, he got out his sheets on "How to Handle Basketball Players" and changed each one.

That story that day, coupled with four years of observation, is perhaps the most important thing I learned while at UCLA. Earlier in my coaching career I used to consider it a challenge when I had a problem with an athlete. "I can handle him," I would always think to myself. I no longer try to "handle" players. I try very hard to understand them and their problems, and then work with them to solve it in the best interest of both the team and the young man.

The daily staff meetings were frequently spiced with Coach Wooden's "words of wisdom" or "pearls of great price." Each time he made a comment of particular significance to me, I made a special point of writing it down in my practice plan notebook to keep for future reference and study.

One such pearl occurred during the first week of practice. We were discussing which combination of players we should put together during our early scrimmages as the players were exhibiting their talents in an effort to make the playing squad. Coach Wooden explained that he always gave the experienced players more time to prove themselves during the early practices. It was the responsibility of the younger players to prove themselves good enough over an extended period of time to take away a starting position, if they were able. By giving the veterans the first options at the starting unit, Coach Wooden felt they would have no legitimate complaint if a younger player beat them out in time. It was obvious to me that internal dissension was kept at an absolute minimum by adhering to this philosophy.

A solemn bench prior to the 1975 NCAA championship game against Kentucky. This was to be Coach Wooden's final game.

In our first team meeting, Coach Wooden explained to the players that he would, in time, select a starting lineup and two, possibly three, first-line substitutes as his playing squad. The remaining four or five members on our twelve-man squad were told then and there that they would not see game action until it was obvious that we would win or lose the game. He expected these players to either accept these rules or resign their position from the team.

When I questioned Coach Wooden further about this mandate the first week of practice, he explained some additional interesting concepts to me. He consistently would play only those players who exhibited a good attitude and who were producing. He was strong in his conviction to not play players who had potential but displayed poor attitudes. There was no room for a selfish player in his program.

When I inquired how he expected to keep the non-playing squad members happy, his answer was twofold. First, it was not his responsibility to try to keep them happy. He believed it was a distinct privilege to be a member of the UCLA squad, and it was the responsibility of the players to keep themselves in a positive mental attitude for the best interest of the team. Second, he felt this was easily accomplished by identifying each player's role and by wise selection of his squad members. By that, he meant that the last four or five players on the squad should be selected on the basis of their practice ability and positive attitudes. They were not necessarily the best players in rank order that tried out for the squad.

My questions were then directed to the starting five and the two or three primary substitutes. How did he determine who would start? How many subs, two or three? When did he make the decision? Would he ever change the lineups? If so, when?

His answers were as varied as my questions. Most fans, he explained, generally have their own opinion as to who should start and which combination should play. Ninety percent of the time their decisions are based on offensive ability. A professional coach must not fall into that trap. He must first of all determine which components make up his brand of basketball. At UCLA there were four major areas of emphasis: (1) half court offense, (2) half court defense, (3) fast break, and (4) full court press. Coach's formula for selecting his playing squad included all four categories plus a fifth—team play.

After allowing each player an opportunity to exhibit his wares (usually three to four weeks), Coach and his two assistants would meet to determine the starting lineup. Each would take a paper and pencil, and without collaborating with the others, they would itemize the following:

1. List the five best half court offensive players.
2. List the five best half court defensive players.
3. List the five best fast breaking players (this includes rebounding as well as speed, dribbling, and passing ability).
4. List the five best full court pressure players (this includes quickness, anticipation, etc.).
5. List the five players who play together the best as a team.

Coach Wooden was of the opinion that some players did not play well with others. He strived to choose players who could play well as a unit. More often than not his starting lineup was made up of the five that could play together the best, rather than the five best players in rank order.

After we completed our lists separately, we tabulated them. Coach believed that his playing squad should consist of those players whose names appeared on the lists most frequently. If a player's name was on all five lists consistently, surely he would be a starter. If his name was on four of the lists, he would more than likely be a starter also. It was common for several players to be on three of the five consistently. When that was the case, we would look for those players whose names were on the "team player" list. That would normally be the determining factor. I found the formula to be a very objective way to determine playing groups. There were occasionally some interesting surprises.

The validity of this system is best illustrated the year that Bill Walton and Swen Nater were both playing for us. Swen was our 7 ft 0, 245 pound backup center and one of the best shooters on our team. He never started a game at UCLA, and yet during his rookie season in the ABA he was selected rookie of the year. In 1979-80, he was the leading rebounder in the NBA. The UCLA fans continually "suggested" to Coach Wooden that he start both Walton and Nater. But Coach stuck to his guns and would not deviate from his formula. He justified his stand by pointing out that if Bill and Swen played together we would probably be a better offensive team, but our defense, fast break, and full court press would all suffer. It was really obvious to me that his wisdom was much greater than that of many of our fans.

Coach preferred to have only two substitutes: One for the guards, and one for the forwards and center. However, if we had an outstanding player such as Nater who was a pure center and could play no other position, then Coach would have three main subs, one for the guards, one for the forwards, and one for the center. Thus, our playing squad consisted of seven or eight players.

As I mentioned previously, Coach Wooden believed in taking a reasonable length of time before determining who would start, who would sub, and who would sit. Once that judgment had been made, changes were far and few between. Each year it seemed as if Gary would try to get Coach Wooden to give a player or two an additional opportunity to play more as the season progressed. Coach Wooden would chide him, "Gary, you're too soft-hearted; I will not change personnel just to give a sub a chance to prove himself. He already has had his opportunity." From the success that Gary enjoyed the two years he coached UCLA, I would say that he learned the lesson well.

Wooden used to explain that it took a great deal of consideration and patience to decide who should play, and it would take equal time and patience before he made a change. The players could then feel secure in their positions and know that one bad ball game or weekend would not put them on the bench. They consistently played better as a result of their sense of security. On the other hand, if they played poorly for two or three consecutive weeks, then a change was in order, and it was made without reservation.

If we ever suggested to Coach Wooden that we prepare for the unexpected such as a special defense against us, or perhaps an injury to a key player, he would counsel us, "Do not prepare for adversity in advance. Prepare positively for your strength—then if the unexpected occurs, change if necessary."

On occasion we would have a player who would get his nose out of joint. I would then remember Coach's advice to not let our emotions affect our comments to players. Criticize, but do not belittle a player. Do not be sarcastic, cute, or cut a person with wit. Scold him for his actions, for not being businesslike, but do not cut him down in front of his peers. This advice went hand-in-hand in working with players instead of handling them.

When a player made a mistake, Coach would suggest that a mistake could be beneficial if he would do four things with it: (1) recognize it, (2) admit it, (3) learn from it, and (4) forget it.

During our practice session, Coach employed several little "gimmicks" to keep the enthusiasm of all the players at a high plain. When we were involved in fundamentals and break-down drills, he would mix the players. Once team-oriented drills commenced, however, he would keep the playing group of seven or eight together. They were never allowed to compete against each other in five-on-five situations.

He felt that the subs' attitudes usually regressed somewhat when these team-oriented drills began. He would, therefore, delay team situations for as long as possible. Each day we concluded practice with a five-on-five controlled scrimmage. The top seven would always play as a unit against the non-playing group. We would alternate from offense to defense. The coaching staff directed their entire attention to the top unit. Little attention was given to the non-playing group, as the emphasis was geared to preparing the main group for combat. To keep the non-playing unit motivated as much as possible, Coach would usually put them on offense first. That seemed to keep the "up" and their defense usually followed suit.

In the four years I assisted at UCLA we won 115 and lost 7. For that reason, I had little opportunity to observe another of Coach Wooden's coaching tips. He would suggest to us that when his teams were playing well and winning, he would be "on them" more than when they were losing. He would admonish us not to ride a team when it was losing. Rather, it would be wiser to analyze and work the team hard, but not chide the players.

We were in our second practice of the year when I had my first opportunity to see Coach Wooden put into practice the manner in which he worked with his players. A potential internal dissension problem was quickly changed to a positive feeling of team unity.

Early in the practice during our fast break and fundamental drills, Gary was stationed under one basket and I was stationed under the other. Coach Wooden was observing the drills from a chair on the sideline at half court. Bill Walton was a sophomore. Greg Lee was his closest friend and also a sophomore. Gary and I each noticed that Bill and Greg were having a particularly enjoyable time taking "cheap shots" at a third player, Gary Franklin. He was a former high school teammate of Greg's. The comments were quiet and subtle, but nevertheless very cutting.

At the conclusion of practice, the players were instructed to shoot free throws. Gary and I sat down with Coach and commented to him about the goings-on between Bill, Greg and Gary. After hearing us out, Coach blew his whistle and called the players together around him. Gary and I arose and stood behind the players. Coach Wooden proceeded to talk to the players about the great civilizations that ruled the world in times past. He made the analogy that throughout the history of mankind whenever a great civilization fell, it crumbled from within. He cited the example of how the internal problems of the Roman Empire and others caused their demise. He concluded by

saying that our team had the potential of being one of the great
basketball teams in the country that year. He expressed his belief that
the only thing that could keep us from being a great team would be
ourselves. We must care for each other, understand and respect our
differences and individuality and work collectively for a common goal.
We must not crumble from within.

As he spoke, I kept my eyes focused on Bill and Greg. They both
nodded in agreement as Coach made his point. When the team was
dismissed, both of them walked to Gary on the way to the locker room
and apologized for their actions of that day.

That was the last incident we had that entire year concerning a
lack of togetherness. We went on to a 30-0 season and the NCAA
championship.

*At the press conference following the 1973
championship in St. Louis.*

To me, that was the first, but certainly not the last time I witnessed
Coach Wooden's uncanny ability to say the right thing at the right
time. He was an absolutely eloquent public speaker. During our four
years at UCLA, Bee and I had the opportunity of spending many an
evening at some gala occasions honoring Coach Wooden. His public
addresses, his acceptance speeches, and other occasional addresses
were always delivered in a most interesting and entertaining manner.
Whether Coach had an audience of one or a thousand, he felt at home.

The first summer we were together, Gary and I worked with Coach in his former basketball summer camps at Palisades High School. At lunch time we would sit with several other coaches in the locker room and visit. As one would imagine, Coach Wooden was soon on center stage. Shortly after Coach started telling stories, Gary would politely excuse himself and leave. I couldn't understand why, because personally, I was intrigued. One day I inquired of Gary why he would always leave. He smiled and explained that he had been with Coach Wooden for over 10 years and had already heard all of his stories on more than one occasion. A couple of years later, Gary and I would both excuse ourselves.

Perhaps the occasions that impressed me the greatest were his comments to our players during the games. His pre-game, half-time and post-game comments were always magnificant. His demeanor was calm and confident. I'll never forget the night of the first NCAA championship game I was involved with. It was against Florida State in the L.A. Sports Arena in March 1972. I was as nervous as an expectant father, as were several of the players. When Coach walked in, his poised, positive pre-game presentation calmed all of us. He seemed to be at his very best at the most important games.

In the four years I was his assistant, I never heard him use the word "WIN" during a game. Not before, during, nor after. He would always admonish our players to do their best. "And if you do," he would say, "you will more than likely be pleased with the final score."

It was easy for me to see why young prospects would want to play for Coach Wooden. His many years of experience had enabled him to develop a perfect blend of coaching brilliance and genuine concern for his players. As his chief recruiter, I found that the door was always open to me when, as his assistant, I introduced myself to a prospect.

I mentioned earlier his ruling regarding out-of-state prospects. Quite often he would bring letters into my office from young men who had written to him expressing an interest in UCLA. Some of them were so unique that I soon started a file of "Interesting Letters" that I have maintained since. I would like to share a few of them.

A typical letter:

Dear Coach,

I am writing to you because I am a highschool basketball player. I am a 6'2" guard, and this will be my senior year in high school.

I would like to know if you scout this area for players, and I would appreciate any answer you could give me. I've enclosed a self-addressed, stamped envelope for your convenience. Thank you.

Sincerely,

A not so typical letter:

Dear John Wooden

I will be coming to U.C.L.A as soon you send me a plane ticket.

Love

A letter from a young man who is in for a rude awakening:

Jan/4/74
Houston, Mo 65483

Dear Franks H. Arnold

What kinds of course do you think i take to go out for basketball, football, and baseball, i would like to go out for athletics, how do you get a collar ship or grant-in-aid to go to U-C-L-A,

Sincerely

A letter from a confident young man from Brooklyn, New York:

Mr. Frank Arnold
University of California, Los Angeles
405 Hilgard Avenue
Los Angeles, California 90024

Brooklyn, New York,
September 5, 1972

Dear Mr. Arnold,

I am writing in reference to the questionaire I sent you. I really desire to play for your school. I have letters form every school in the nations', but I want to play for U.C.L.A. right now I can shoot better than any wing man you have on your team now.

I played on a game this year and hit 71 pts. and missed only 8 field goals attempts. There is no defense zone or other wise that can stop me. from scoring. This year I avg. 38.9 my team went 20-3. I have just returned from five-star basketball camp, I made second team all-prep. This year I am a pre-season all-american. If you come hear you will not be sorry, out come.

Looking forward to seeing you.

A letter from a young man from Kentucky who admired Sidney Wicks:

Cumberland, Kentucky

Dear Mr Wooden,

All my life in been looking
at UCLA and one day I hope that
I will come to UCLA. one thing I
can do I have the ability at both
end of the floor. I play for Cumberland
High school scorer about 21 point
game rebounder 14.9 a game I jumper
like a 6.8 but just 6.1 been look
how many NCAA championship you
have win. want I was just a
little but been want to go to your
college all my life this why ask
you please come next year and
see me I just junior this year
but next year will be senar. I like
see Sidney Wicks play like
his style. people in Cumberland
call me Wick because have the
ability on the floor like to walk
back and forward like to glare
around like conton the floor before
played. ?   Your Truely

After the 1971 NCAA championship game when UCLA defeated Villanova, a tall, slender young man somehow worked his way into the Bruin dressing room at the Astrodome in Houston. He introduced himself and expressed his interest in playing for Coach Wooden after he graduated the following year. Denny Crum took his name and address down and promised to contact him the next year. Denny, of course, left for Louisville shortly thereafter, and I replaced him. When I arrived on campus in June, Gary told me about the young man, but we could find no trace of him in the files Denny left behind. All Gary could remember was that he came from a small high school in western Louisiana. I spent several weeks tracking him down and finally came up with a 6 ft 11 in player from Lake Charles, Louisiana, who in fact had been in Houston for the championship game. I wrote him a letter; here is his reply:

W O Boston High

Dear Coach

I was very happy to hear from you as I took out time to write this letter. coach I am from a family of 14. we are 12 living 4 boys and eight girls. I began playing basketball in the eight grade. My average was about 32 points a game. Rebounding ave about 15--- or 20 a game. My first year in high school I make the first team We went to state the year after I was rule ineligible, I will not go in to it coach, for it is a long story. This set me back but I contented playing with the boys. It was very hard to set out a whole year and watch my school team get beat They did not do well that year but the next year for 70-71 basketball we went to state. I set a records in rebounds hauling down 30. coach I have a lot to learn about basketball. Coach I will not lie to any body about my grades. I am not bright I have a D-C average which is not very good my average is better in some think. Coach I could go on all night but I will stop here. I hope you can help me out. If not it was good while it lasted coach. Coach I am only 6 ft 11 weigh 197 pounds.

                    Sincerely yours,

    That was easily the saddest letter I ever received. He obviously needed additional help academically—it would be impossible for us to have him admitted at UCLA. My heart went out to the young man in hope that someday he could get a college education and be successful in life. As it worked out, he eventually enrolled in a small college in the south and is now playing in the NBA.

On a lazy summer day in June, things were rather slow at the office when Gary and I got into a discussion about the different kinds of prospects and their parents that we had encountered over the years. We had a few good laughs over some of the letters I had in my file. About thirty minutes after our conversation, the secretary brought in the afternoon mail. Lo and behold, another letter from a "suspect.":

Dear Coach Armailed :

I really like to play UCLA. I'm the best play in my area and in the United States. I'm A student and an 6' 9" inches height. I score 32 points a game last year and averaged 14 rebees game. I shoot all over - outside, inside & middle. Me good defense and I block ten shots each game.

If any way I can go to UCLA I will. I am senior this year at Poot High. I have over 100 schools interested me. Please help me to come UCLA.

Yours in Sports,

Truebell Alton

P.S. my only fault is that I lie a little

When I read the P.S. I knew I had been had. I chased down Gary and found him having another good laugh at my expense. He was the illustrious Truebell Alton.

UCLA basketball games, particularly NCAA tournament play are a part of history. It is not my desire to repeat what has already been written about so extensively. The final four championship tournament was, of course, the highlight of each year.

The first tournament I was involved in was played at the Sports Arena in Los Angeles in March 1972. We beat Louisville and Florida State for the championship. I recall mostly the carnival atmosphere of the press and the enthusiastic support of the boosters of the respective teams.

My first gold watch—Coach Wooden-s eighth.

The 1972-73 season we played Indiana in the semifinals and Memphis State for the championship. The tournament was held in St. Louis. The Memphis game was the night Walton shot 22 times and made 21. Not a bad night's work.

After the game, one of our super boosters, Harry Guss, took a group of about 20 people, including the coaches, A.D., the university chancellor, and all the wives to an exclusive restaurant on the banks of the Mississippi River for a celebration dinner. The bill must have been astronomical. It was a tradition with Harry to treat this group after a

UCLA 1973 NCAA Champions
30-0   75 Consecutive Wins

My second gold watch—Coach Wooden's ninth.

One second to play—UCLA 87 Memphis State 66.

NCAA crown. At the beginning of the season, Harry always gave each of the coaches a half dozen pair of dress socks. On the way back to the Final Four tournament, he would give each of us an expensive silk tie and a silver dollar encased in a special holder with an inscription that read, "To Coach Frank Arnold-UCLA 1973-From Harry Guss-with 'MAZEL' ". At the sight of the tournament he would always take the coaches' wives on a shopping spree and buy them a spring outfit. Harry was, indeed, a very generous man.

At one of many special banquets honoring Coach Wooden. He stands between Tom Harmon and Harry Guss. Dick Enberg is on my right and Eddie Einhorn of TVS is on Gary's left.

The third year, March 1974, we played in the Sports Arena at Greensboro, North Carolina. Our opponent in the semi-final games was North Carolina State. They beat us in double overtime, 80-77. An unusual thing occurred in this game that few people know about. At the time it was quite alarming, but it can now be looked upon as a rather humorous incident!

At half the score was 35-35. The regulation game ended at 65-65. As you can imagine, it was a great game filled with one pressure situation after another. With a little over one minute to play in the first overtime, we clled for time-out. The score was 75-75. When the horn sounded to resume play, we took our seats on the bench. As I sat down, Gary was on his hands and knees in front of me working his way back to his seat. I assumed he had lost his contact lens, so I instructed some of the players sitting next to me to help Coach Cunningham look for them. As Gary took his seat, I ribbed him, "Shucks, Gary, there's got to be an easier way to get on National T.V. than looking for your contacts on all fours." He looked up at me with an ashen white face and responded in almost a whisper, "I haven't lost my contacts, Frank, I fainted." It was very obvious to me then that Gary was not well. We were to find out after the game that his body had simply dehydrated, which, in turn, caused him to pass out.

The first overtime ended 77-77. We literally helped Gary into the team huddle and back. After a couple more "shaky" time-outs and a second overtime, we eventually lost our first NCAA tournament game after 38 consecutive tournament victories.

After the game, we had the team doctor attend to Gary, and he was soon back on his feet. In the interim, though, I had to go to the rescue of one of the ushers in charge of crowd control near the players' dressing areas. Gary's wife, Barbara, had detected something was wrong with her husband and had headed for our quarters at the conclusion of the game. The usher had been instructed by his supervisor to allow absolutely no one into the area without a pass. When he tried to stop Barbara, he met his match. She was not to be denied. I believe I arrived on the scene just in time to save his life.

My final year at UCLA was also to be John Wooden's final year as a coach. It culminated in storybook fashion at San Diego in March 1975. In the semi-finals we made a historic comeback to defeat Louisville 75-74 in overtime. After the game, Wooden announced his retirement. There were many tears shed in the locker room.

When we took the floor for the championship game against Kentucky, there was a lump in the throat and a tear in the eye of every UCLA fan in the arena, including mine. It was a very somber pre-game warmup. The game was a barn burner, however. We eventually won 92-88. It was all over. The John Wooden Era had concluded in spectacular fashion, and with it the greatest dynasty in sports history.

7

HEAD COACH

For assistant basketball coaches, spring fever often carries a unique virus. It's called "head coachitus." Each spring the bug to get a head coaching position strikes a good number of assistants nationwide. Coaches by nature are not only competitive, but egocentric. Their ego trip is to be their own boss—to do their own thing.

I was no exception. After a couple of years at UCLA, I had a strong urge to become a head coach at a major university. Being one of Coach Wooden's assistants was a real asset. I had been privileged to have very attractive financial offers to accept head coaching positions at three prestigious institutions, plus feelers from a couple others. Had I not been at UCLA, I would have accepted any of the three. The fact that I was one of Wooden's proteges, however, made it possible for me to be a bit choosey. I was determined to accept a job only if it met two criteria. First, it had to be in a geographic region where my wife and I would feel comfortable rearing our children. Second, the university must have the potential of becoming a nationally prominent basketball program. None of the schools we visited satisfied both criteria, so we declined the invitations. After doing so, I sometimes shook my head in bewilderment.

One university in the south offered me a particularly lucrative deal. During the two-day interview with the athletic director, for breakfast he took me to the plantation home of their biggest booster. We were served by six white-coated butlers. The southern host was a multi-millionaire. He told the athletic director in my presence to "hire this young man at all costs." The package they eventually offered me included a very lucrative salary. We were to choose our home, and they would make the payments (while I was with the AD, Bee was being shown homes by a real estate lady), two cars, fifteen TV shows of a minimum of $750 per show, and two to four weeks of summer camp, from which I could keep all the profits. The total package neared $100,000 per year.

In January, 1975, I received a long-distance telephone call from an old friend of mine who lived in Salt Lake City. His son had been a member of the Brigham Young University team. He asked if I would be interested in the head coaching job at BYU. I was surprised by his inquiry and asked if the coach had resigned. He told me he had not, but speculation was that he might at the end of the year. With that, I told the gentleman that the BYU coach, Glen Potter, was a friend of mine and that I wouldn't even consider discussing the job possibility while he was still coaching. That was the end of our conversation. As the months passed, I had an occasional call from other people in Salt Lake and Provo, indicating that rumor was growing stronger that Potter might resign and that my name, along with a few others, was being mentioned as a possible replacement. As usual, my answer was that I would not discuss the position until if and when Potter did, in fact, step down. I must confess, however, that the possibility of coaching at BYU intrigued me far more than any other head job in America. I had a special fondness in my heart for Provo and BYU. I met my wife at BYU, we were married in Salt Lake, and had our first two children while living in Provo. It was not my original home, but I claimed it as such, for the five years I lived in Provo were particuarly special to me.

We did not get our hopes too high, however. As fate would have it, the three other major colleges in Utah had all had coaching changes within the last 24 months. I would have been pleased and proud to have become the head coach at any of the three: Utah State, Weber State, and the University of Utah. As each coach resigned, I quickly inquired about the position. In each case, however, the job never opened, because the assistant coach at each school was awarded the head job. Utah is a state rich in basketball tradition—BYU would be the last possibility in our favorite state for years to come. For Frank Arnold, it would be the ultimate choice.

During the week of March 3, I received three very interesting phone calls. The first was from the athletic director's office at San Diego State University. The head coaching job had been open for about a month. The call was to inform me that I had been selected as one of the four finalists. They requested that I travel to San Diego for an interview. I explained that I wanted to talk to my wife about it first, and that I would get back to them. Bee and I discussed the possibility at length, and decided to go for the interview. The next day I returned the call and accepted the invitation. I expressed that I wanted to be the last candidate to be interviewed. They agreed to that, and we set the session up for the following Thursday, March 13, at 10 a.m.

Later that week I received the second call shortly after arriving home. It was from a man who lived in Provo. He explained to me that within the last hour Potter had returned from the President's office where he had handed in his resignation. It was to be announced the first part of next week. The purpose of the call was to inform me that this particular fellow would use his limited influence to get me the job, if I would consider him as an assistant. (I did not hire him.)

The next day I received another call from Provo. This time it was the Dean of Physical Education at BYU, Dr. Clayne Jensen. My heart skipped three beats when he introduced himself. He explained that Coach Potter had resigned and that the administration wanted to act swiftly in hiring a replacement. As he put it, I was one of "two or three candidates" that they were interested in. He inquired as to my interest and whether I would be able to travel to Salt Lake and Provo for interviews. I quickly assured him that I was, and that I could.

We set the interview for 9 a.m. on Wednesday, March 12, at the Hotel Utah in Salt Lake City. He then cautioned me to come in absolute confidency. They were very anxious to hold private interviews with no news leaks whatsoever.

The next few days were very hectic indeed. I loaded every gun I had at my disposal to prepare for the battle ahead. I sought advice from key people: John Wooden, J.D. Morgan, Gary Cunningham, Frankie Moore, my bishop and my stake president. I called several intimate friends in Salt Lake and Provo to seek their advice and support. Dr. Milton H. Hartvigsen, the former dean of the BYU College of Physical Education and Athletics, played an instrumental role in advising and helping me. Sunday night I began a three-day fast that was concluded at lunch during the interview itself.

When I left the office Tuesday afternoon, I told my secretary to tell people who called for me that I was on my way to San Diego, and wouldn't return until Friday. That was partially true, because I had the appointment for the San Diego State interview Thursday morning.

I flew to Salt Lake and was met at the airport by a very close personal friend, Arlen Crouch. I was to stay at his home that evening. When we arrived at his house, his wife, Derrell, showed me the sports section of that evenings' "Deseret News." The headlines read: Y: POTTER OUT; ANDY IN? The reference was to Ladell Anderson, the former Utah State University and Utah Stars ABA team head coach. He is currently the athletic director at Utah State and one of the most popular and highly-respected gentlemen and coaches in the business. My heart sank as I read how he was a leading candidate and had been on the BYU campus all day Tuesday for his interview. It was obvious that I had neither the reputation nor experience of Ladell. Nevertheless, I was determined in my efforts and prepared to give it my best shot.

The next morning Arlen drove me to the Hotel Utah. I walked into the lobby at 9 a.m. and looked for Dr. Jensen. He was nowhere in sight. I took a seat assuming he and his party would enter shortly. By 9:15 there was still no Dr. Jensen. I began to wonder if my interview was simply a political one and if they had, in fact, offered the position to Ladell. I was relieved when at 9:20 Dr. Jensen walked in along with President Dallin H. Oaks and Vice-President Ben E. Lewis. They had simply been delayed in traffic during their trip from Provo.

We went to a suite in the hotel they had reserved for our meeting. After a few minutes of exchanging pleasantries, President Oaks began to speak of the importance of the position of head basketball coach at Brigham Young University. He told of the image of the program, the example the coaches and players must set, and the importance of being successful. For over one hour I listened intently as he explained virtually every facet of the program

At the conclusion of his remarks, he asked if I had any questions or if there was anything that I cared to say. "Yes, sir, there is." I responded. For the next sixty minutes I explained to the President and his two associates my feelings about the job, what I felt had to be accomplished, and how I would go about the task if selected. As I spoke I felt enough confidence to make my point in such a manner that I sensed that the three gentlemen were deeply interested in what I had to say.

When I finished, lunch was served and we exchanged questions and answers for the next hour. They then asked me to leave the room for a few minutes while they sat in private consultation. I felt good about the events of the last three hours. Nevertheless, I was quite nervous as I paced the hallways for the next fifteen or twenty minutes.

They called me back and indicated to me that they now wanted me to walk with them the one half block to the LDS Church Administration Building. Having worked for BYU before as a coach at BY High School, I knew that no faculty member was hired until he had been interviewed by one of the general authorities of the Church. It was a good sign.

I was introduced first to some members of the Church Board of Education. As we visited, one of the members suggested that if I was hired he could give me some good news and some bad news. I asked what the good news was.

He responded, "You will have everyone coming back" (referring, of course, to the players).

I then asked what the bad news was.

"You will have everyone coming back."

During the next hour I was to visit with a total of five general authorities, concluding with a formal interview with Marvin J. Ashton. After each brief interview, the general authorities, President Oaks and his party would go off into a corner somewhere and confer for a few minutes. It was obvious to me that I was getting a good looking-over.

We next adjourned to the Church Office Building, where I was introduced to the Commissioner of Church Education, Neal A. Maxwell. Once again the group met for a few minutes after his visit with me.

President Oaks then asked me if I could get a car and follow them to the BYU campus in Provo. They wanted me to meet with Stan Watts, who was at the time the athletic director. Stan was unable to meet with us in Salt Lake because of a temporary problem with his eyes. Arlen Crouch had already offered the use of his wife's car, so I assured them I could.

After a very pleasant meeting with Stan, during which we discussed the basketball scene in more depth, Dr. Jensen asked me to follow them to the administration building for another session with the President. He explained to me, however, that I must not be seen with him or Stan or any other BYU administrator. He told me to park my car in the parking lot and enter the side door of the administration building and walk directly to the President's office on the third floor. They wanted to keep my presence on campus as confidential as possible.

I parked according to his instructions and walked to the side door of the A.O. Smoot Administration building. It was locked. Dr. Jensen and Stan were on the front sidewalk about 75 yards ahead of me. I waited until they entered the front door and then followed them as inconspicuously as possible. I felt a bit foolish with this cloak-and-dagger operation, but understood their concern and need for secrecy.

It was 7 p.m. Ben Lewis met me on the third floor and ushered me into his office. He asked me to wait there until they called for me. The thirty minutes I waited seemed like an eternity. One can imagine the anxiety as I wondered what the future had in store. Would I be offered the job I wanted more than any other position in the world, or would I have to take the 7 a.m. flight to San Diego the next morning?

The door opened, and Ben Lewis asked me to walk with him to the President's office. This was it. President Oaks, Dr. Jensen, and Stan Watts were waiting for us. I sat down. President Oaks spoke. "Frank, you have met with the four of us at length today, and six general authorities. I want you to know at this time that to the man we unanimously agree that we would like you to be the new head basketball coach at Brigham Young University."

A greater sense of humility I have never felt. I was virtually speechless. A lump was in my throat, and tears swelled in my eyes as I managed to utter, "Thank you, I am grateful to each of you—I accept."

I immediately called my wife as she shared the same feelings I did about BYU and her home town of Provo.

The next morning, Thursday, March 13, 1975, we held a press conference at 8:30 a.m. to announce the appointment. At 9:30 we concluded and I rushed to a phone. I placed a long distance telephone call to the athletic director at San Diego State to inform them that I would be unable to make the 10:00 interview.

Press Conference at which I was introduced as the new head basketball coach at BYU.

For the next three weeks I wore two hats: One as head coach at BYU, and one as an assistant at UCLA. UCLA was in the NCAA playoffs, and I was obligated to finish the season with them. There were very few problems involved in fulfilling both assignments, just more hours of work.

One problem did occur during the Regional Playoffs. The Bruins were playing in the Western Regionals at Tempe, Arizona. I was assigned to scout the Mid-West Regionals at Las Cruces, New Mexico, from which our opponents in the NCAA Final Four championship would come. That same weekend the Utah State High School 4-A championship tournament was being held in Salt Lake City. There was a senior named Craig Christensen, a junior named Scott Runia, and a sophomore named Danny Vranes that I very much wanted to see play.

Cincinnati was to play Louisville, and Maryland vs. Notre Dame on Thursday night at Las Cruces. The winners were to play for the championship Saturday afternoon. If UCLA won the Western Regionals, we would play the winner of the Mid West Regional in San Diego at the NCAA championships. I had worked out a flight schedule which would allow me to see Thursday's games in Las Cruces, fly to Salt Lake early Friday morning to see the high school state tournament that night, leave at 6 a.m. Saturday morning, and be back in Las Cruces in time to see the afternoon championship game.

Everything went very smoothly until Saturday morning. As I drove to the Salt Lake City Airport at 5:30 a.m., a slight snow began to fall. When I boarded the plane at 5:50, it was snowing very heavily. At 6:00, which was the scheduled departure time, the captain announced over the P.A. system that we would have to wait for a few minutes while the snow plows cleared the runway. The snow fell so abundantly that thirty minutes later the flight was cancelled. Therefore, I was going to miss the second round of the regionals.

I called Wooden to explain my dilemma. His main concern was whether or not I had a good report of each of the teams. I felt I did, and reassured him of such. Wooden understood, but J.D. Morgan was more than a little disturbed about my side trip. As it worked out, Louisville won the Mid-West championship and UCLA won the West championship. We then played Louisville in the first round in San Diego and won in an overtime 75-74. I don't care to think of what J.D. Morgan would have said to me had we lost.

It has been said that the major difference between being an assistant coach and being a head coach is making suggestions instead of making decisions. I very quickly found that to be true. It was easy to make suggestions during the ten years I served as an assistant coach. The ultimate decision lies in the hands of the head coach, however, and certain decisions are sometimes very difficult to make. When I became the head coach at Brigham Young University, I was soon confronted with the unfamiliar task of making important decisions on a daily basis.

Decisions tend to fall into one of three categories. The first is the every day decision pertaining to the daily routine of coaching (i.e., job description for assistant coaches, equipment and supply purchases, practice plans including drills, recruiting, public relations, academic coordination, etc.). These decisions are, for the most part, easy to make, with little concern on the part of others.

The second category, however, seems to be of great concern to everyone. These decisions occur during the game and pertain to the strategy involved as the game unfolds. The head coach receives substantial help from the fans pertaining to these matters. Unfortunately, most of the help comes after the fact. Although the outcome of the game often rides on the decisions that are made, most coaches feel very comfortable in having to make them. More often than not they have to be made at the spur of the moment, but the head coach, better than anyone else, is capable and ready to make that decision. He is a professional and makes his decisions based on many years of preparation and study rather than on the emotions of the game that often dictate the advice that he receives from "Joe Fan."

The third category consists of the most difficult of all decisions to make. These are the "people-oriented" decisions—decisions that can affect the lives of young men. They begin with those whom a coach chooses to recruit, continues with decisions pertaining to whom should be kept on the squad, who should start the game, when and for whom substitutes should be made, at what point a starter should be replaced in the starting lineup, what actions require disciplinary measures, and what the discipline—probation, suspension or elimination—should be.

I have not met one coach in my entire lifetime that has not confessed that these "people" decisions have caused him anguish and heartache every year. They are not easy decisions to make, because they "hurt" people. But they must be made, and they must be made by the head coach. He will rightfully seek the advice of his assistants and other learned people, but in the end he is the one that must make and live with the decisions. I guess that's why it is often "lonely at the top."

Several such "people" decisions had to be made the first year I was at BYU. I found that the BYU team was made up of some outstanding young men, but some questionable characters and players as well. I met with each player individually. Within the first couple of weeks I had a mutual agreement with four of the players that they would be "more at home" at other universities. Their lifestyles and personal commitments to BYU and its code of honor simply were not compatible. In each case they transferred to other schools without malice for BYU.

One of the returning players was a dual-sport athlete named Gifford Nielsen. He had red-shirted in football his sophomore year and started as guard in basketball. He was 6 feet 5 inches, 210 pounds, and the book on him in football was a potential All-American at quarterback. In basketball the scouts rated him as a great leader, very good shooter, with average quickness and speed.

When Gifford and I met we agreed that his future had so much potential in football that he would be wise to concentrate on that and drop basketball. I personally hated to see such a fine young man with his shooting and leadership qualities leave our program. Nevertheless, it was the wise thing for him to do, and I endorsed his decision.

Later that fall our head football coach, LaVell Edwards, approached me with an interesting proposal. It was on a Wednesday night at an athletic staff social at the Sundance Ski Resort. LaVell asked me if I would be interested in having Gifford rejoin our team by our first day of practice, October 15. I was puzzled and asked why he would allow him to leave the football team early. LaVell explained that Gifford was really struggling in their practice sessions. He further explained that Giff was such an outstanding young man with such a great attitude that he hated to see him practice so long and hard without the reward of playing more. The team had struggled a bit the first few games of the season, and LaVell felt that the scores simply were not sufficient to allow him to give Gifford playing time. As an afterthought, LaVell commented that he couldn't help but wonder if Giff was one of those few players who was a "game player" a player who, although he showed poorly in practice, was really quite productive during the game itself. That type player is very rare, far and few between. "But," he concluded, "we just haven't been in a position to let him prove himself in the games."

We agreed to talk about it again at a later date. The following Saturday evening we were playing the University of New Mexico. At the end of the third quarter, UNM led 15-0. The offense was sputtering. LaVell made a very interesting decision. He inserted Gifford Nielsen into the game. Giff promptly threw two touchdown passes, and we won 16-15. The rest is history. Giff went on to win All-American honors. He was a leading candidate for the Heisman Trophy before being felled with a knee injury half-way through his senior year. He is now a very popular quarterback with the Houston Oilers.

During that initial fall semester my two new assistants and I were very busy implementing a totally new program. The first assistant I hired was Harry Anderson, a very popular and successful high school and JC coach and a former BYU great. I assigned him the responsibility of being our academic coordinator.

My first two BYU assistants, John McMullen and Harry Anderson.

The fellow I hired as our recruiting coordinator was equally as popular and successful in Southern California, John McMullen. The three of us visited the deans and several department chairmen of virtually every college within the university. Our purpose was to be made aware of the strengths and weaknesses of the academic environment at BYU. We were pleased to discover that this great university enjoyed a very positive reputation nationwide for academic excellence. Of particular interest to us was the fact that approximately 85 percent of the BYU faculty held season tickets to the basketball games.

Our administration was equally as supportive, perhaps even more so. President Oaks was probably the biggest fan of all. Each game he was in town he and his wife sat in the first row behind our bench. More often than not he had special guests with him. During the 1975-76 season we were playing the University of Utah, and President Oaks had as his guest the President of the Council of Twelve Apostles of the LDS Church, Ezra Taft Benson, and his wife. It was a great game, and with twelve seconds to play we scored to tie the game. Utah called a time out to set up a last-second play. When the ball was put into play they worked the ball to their best shooter, Jeff Judkins who attempted the last-second shot from about 21 feet out. Our stop-action video tape has since shown that the following events took place:

1. With two seconds on the clock, he caught the ball, shuffled his feet constituting travelling, and initiated his shot.
2. At the highest arch of the ball, the clock expired, showing 0:00 on the clock.
3. On the downward flight their center caught the ball in front of the rim with both hands (thus ending the shot attempt).
4. He lifted the ball over the rim with both hands on the ball, and dropped it through the basket (an illegal basketball interference by rule during those days).

The referee ruled the basket good. The U of U, therefore, was declared the winner, 76-74, and the refs hurried to the dressing room. I didn't need the replay to know that it was an erroneous call, costing us the game. (Although I didn't realize he had travelled until I saw the video later.) I bolted from the bench absolutely enraged by the call. I hadn't taken two steps onto the floor before I had my suit coat off and gave it a heave towards our bench. It was a bitter, but helpless feeling, since I felt cheated but realized there was nothing that could be done. About that very moment I felt a strong hand on my shirt-sleeved shoulder. I turned and was confronted by this graying, elderly gentleman almost as upset as me with a barrage of questions. "They can't do that, can they? The basket shouldn't count, should it? What are you going to do?" It was President Ezra Taft Benson. As quickly as I had angered I attempted to regain my composure and assured him that there was nothing that we could do and that we had, in fact, lost the game. As I spoke I realized that I didn't have my coat, and I was very embarrassed and sheepish as I tried to retrieve it as unnoticeably as possible. I felt a sense of comfort that a man of his stature was "real," that he had emotions and that he was as supportive as he was and has since been.

A long night....

The first couple of years at BYU were, to say the least, interesting. We had some fine young men in the program, but the talent level as a whole was sorely lacking. Our schedule had us playing an average of twelve home games per year, and fifteen away games. We were playing the likes of the University of North Carolina, UCLA, Texas, Illinois, St. John's—all away games as well as the outstanding teams in our conference. Our win loss record suffered proportionately.

My relationship with a few members of the media was of concern to me. For ten years as an assistant I studied Belko and Wooden carefully as they fielded questions. I had always had a very positive relationship with the sports writers and sports casters in both Oregon and Los Angeles. It was a new and different experience as the head coach, however. I was not prepared for the sudden, sharp, pointed questions that some directed toward me. I was particularly not prepared to answer these blunt questions after a difficult loss when my emotions were still high.

I learned some hard lessons the hard way. I learned that if a coach is candid and says how he honestly feels 100 percent of the time, the press can be brutal. I, therefore, learned what head coaches nationwide inevitably learn in time—it's a *game* when being interviewed by some members of the press—and the public are the losers. Some writers and announcers have a difficult time reporting the intent and true meaning of a coach or player's statement accurately. Fortunately, the vast majority of the media are very fair and accurate. But there is a certain percentage that distort meaning more often than not.

Because they do, coaches tend to make "political" statements of no meaning and no value for these reporters.

To better illustrate what I'm trying to say, let me share an article written by a sportswriter from Louisville, Kentucky. This incident occurred to me while on a scouting assignment at Ames, Iowa for the mid-east regionals in 1972. I was at UCLA at the time.

Dateline: S'port—

One Frank Arnold
Tells It Like It Is

By Rick Woodson

I'll never forget the day I interviewed Frank Arnold.
And neither will he.

FRANK ARNOLD IS an assistant basketball coach at UCLA and he was in Ames, Iowa, last week scouting possible opponents for the Bruin Invitational, laughingly called the NCAA tournament, which starts Thursday in Los Angeles.

So last Thursday night, before Southwestern lost to Louisville, I found Arnold in Iowa State's Hilton Coliseum and arranged for a telephone interview the next morning.

Now you'll have to admit, that's the logical thing to do, since UCLA basketball coaches don't exactly keep a summer house in Shreveport. And anyway, it was, in college basketball, kinda like an audience with the Pope or something.

About nine the next morning, I called down to the Holiday Inn and asked for Frank Arnold's room — it was No. 100.

"Hello," said Frank.

"Frank, this is Rick Woodson. I'm sorry I'm a little late," I apologized, "I'll try not to keep you too long."

"Oh, that's okay," he said, "no problem."

So far, so good, eh?

USL LOST TO Louisville, 88-84, and Kansas State defeated Texas, 66-55, so I asked: "What did you think of the two games last night and who do you think will win the regional?"

Now, let me explain that usually when you ask a coach a question like that, you can expect an answer like, "Well, they're both fine teams and it just depends on who gets hot," or "Really, it's hard to say," or "I'd rather not answer on the grounds that it might tend to incriminate me."

Not Frank Arnold. "I don't think there's any doubt that Louisville will win, judging from last night's games," Frank stated flatly. "And Southwestern will without the shadow of a doubt work Texas over real bad."

Now, THIS, I thought, is an interview! Wait'll the AP hears what UCLA's assistant coach had to say! Nothing evasive, nothing fancy, just wham! wham! Hit 'em where it hurts!

I WAS SHAKING inside. Chill bumps jumped up on my arms. I could see it now: "Bruin assistant tells it like it is, says Woodson," spread all over Sports Illustrated and Time.

Surely, this was going to be the biggest day in my newspaper life. I could hardly wait for the next question and answer.

"Frank, what makes UCLA so great? I mean, even when they play a poor game, they still win and other teams don't seem to be able to do that. Why?"

And here he came again. "These people psyche everybody out. It's like me playing golf with Arnold Palmer. Even the things I would do well, he's so much better, he would overcome them. They've got everybody 20-0 when the game starts."

Beautiful! Beautiful! But just one thing: "Frank, why do you say 'they;' aren't you actually on the coaching staff?"

His answer was shattering. "Lord, no!" he laughed. "I'm from Louisville, just a fan here for the tournament."

AT FIRST I THOUGHT he was joking. Then I thought I might be dreaming. Maybe I'm hallucinating!

"You're kidding," I asked weakly.

He wasn't.

I was the victim of an impossible twist of fate. The other Frank Arnold, the one from Los Angeles, was in room 138. If you can, figure the odds on two guys named Frank Arnold, one from Kentucky, one from California, meeting at the same motel on the same day in Ames, Iowa. It's frightening!

Frank Arnold of Kentucky owns a heating and air conditioning business in Louiseville. He graduated from the University of Louisville in 1947 and lives and dies with the Cardinals. He took his family to Iowa and he'll take them to L.A. this week for the Cards' Thursday game with UCLA.

Frank explained his cooperation with the interview. "I thought you were just getting some fans' reactions," he laughed. "I was just trying to think and answer your questions.

"YOU'LL HAVE TO admit, my predictions came true," he pointed out this week in another telephone conversation. USL beat Texas by 30 points for third place and Louisville led KSU all the way). "I also said I think they (the Cardinals) can beat UCLA and I still think they will. We'll give UCLA a whole handful if we play a full ball game as well as we're capable of playing."

I didn't laugh, either, because now, I believe ANYTHING is possible!

Will the Real Frank Arnold . . .

. . . Please Stand Up?

One former sportswriter was a particular source of contention for me. I felt his articles were so inaccurate and biased that I finally cancelled my subscription to his paper and refused to read it until he was replaced. What galled me most I suppose was that for the two years he covered our games he visited me exactly one time in my office, and sat in on no more than four post-game interviews. His columns were opinionated and self-serving without the decency of giving my players or myself "our day in court." I frankly felt persecuted until I was informed that I was in good company. Over the years this sportswriter had attacked at one time or another every football and basketball coach of every major university in the area.

I must hasten to say that as I have matured in my dealings with the media and as new reporters have been assigned to cover our program, I have felt very good about the professional and fair job of reporting that has been done in recent years. Marion Dunn of the Provo Daily Herald and Dick Rosetta of the Salt Lake Tribune are two writers who have a particular sense of fair play and sensitivity to people. Yet their desire to not purposely hurt people does not stand in the way of their excellent and professional manner of reporting.

Lee Benson, the young sports editor of the Deseret News is not above taking a shot at some people, but when he does, it is often done with wit and in good taste. He has a style, a personality, to his reporting, and I believe he has an outstanding future in front of him.

Paul James, the "Voice of the Cougars" of KSL Radio and Television is a pro among pros. He is simply the best there is at his business.

Bill Marcroft, although his blood is as Ute red as the sweater on Arnie Ferin's back, is one of the fine investigative reporters in the business. He is very thorough and very good at his job. I've often kidded with him that he belongs in "the big city."

The third year at BYU good things began to happen. Harry and John had recruited very affectively and we were slowly replacing those players we had inherited with our own recruits. Our starting lineup consisted of a freshman, Danny Ainge, who was an All-American in three sports at South Eugene High School in Oregon; two sophomores, Scott Runia—All State from West High School in Salt Lake City, and Alan Taylor, the L.A. City AAA Player of the Year from Kennedy High School; and two juniors Glen Roberts who was a walk-on from Bingham High School in Utah that played so well he earned himself a full grant-in-aid, and Keith Rice, our first black player from Mt. Hood Community College near Portland, Oregon.

A few quick comments to Dan Ainge.

We were very young and our schedule was a killer. We ended up 12-18, but things were beginning to happen.

That same year Glen Tuckett was appointed as a Director of Athletics. He soon proved to be one of the finest ADs in the country. The entire athletic department began to flourish under his leadership.

The next year, 1978-79, all the pieces seemed to fall together. John McMullen had an appointment to become the head basketball coach at Santa Monica Junior College in Southern California. He left a fine legacy of recruits behind for us. We hired a new assistant with "fire in his britches" from Clearfield High School, Roger Reid. He brought with him an added dimension that fit into our program like a glove.

Harry and I with our new assistant Roger Reid.

We signed three All-American forwards: Devin Durrant from Provo High School, Fred Roberts from Bingham High School and Steve Trumbo from El Modena High School in Southern California. Devin and Fred played so well they replaced Glen and Keith in the starting lineup. It was particularly hard on the latter two because they were both seniors and had each started every game for us as juniors. Nevertheless, they handled the most difficult situation as well as could be expected. For the first time all of our players were young men that we recruited. We finished the season with a 20-8 record and the WAC championship.

Devin Durrant, Dan Ainge, and Steve Trumbo celebrate after our 96-95 triumph over San Diego State for the 1979 WAC championship.

A very humorous incident occurred at a home game that year. We were involved in a very hotly contested game against UTEP. Late in the first half I stood to protest a call when a ball point pen came flying past my ear and onto the playing floor. Our administration and I had recently had a conversation pertaining to our concern about crowd conduct, particularly objects being thrown by spectators. When the pen flew past me, I was quick to anger and turned to the crowd immediately, instructing one of our ushers to find out who threw the missile and escort him from the game. Our university president, Dallin Oaks, was sitting directly behind our bench. He quickly agreed with me to find the culprit and eject him at once. Within minutes a man in the fourth row was being escorted up the stairs by one of the ushers.

After the game the story unfolded even more. On the way home from the game my wife said to me that she thought that the man ejected may have been a guest of my assistant coach, Harry Anderson and his wife Judy. When I asked why she thought this to be the case, she told me that the man was sitting in one of the Anderson seats. I asked Bee what the man looked like, and she said he was a short, handsome man with black wavy hair. The description fit one of Harry's closest friends, Walt Wellman. I wasn't sure whether to laugh or cry.

I checked with Harry first thing Monday morning, and sure enough, Walt was his guest and he was, in fact, invited to leave the game. As it worked out, Walt had a program rolled up in his hand with his ball point pen clipped over the edge of it. He had been keeping score. When the referee made the questionable call, Walt simply expressed, "Oh, Nuts!" and shook his program with a quick motion of objection across his face as a person instinctively does in such a situation. Little did Walt realize that the thrust of the program propelled the pen from it and onto the floor. When President Oaks and I were demanding the outster of the culprit, Walt was just as adamant in his agreement, sitting up, looking around, and agreeing, "Yeah, throw the bum out." When he reached for his pen, the sudden flash of fear struck him that it was *HIS* pen and that he was the "bad guy." As he was sliding further down into the seat in an attempt to be unnoticed, he saw everyone looking at him as the usher walked toward him. A lady directly behind Walt was pointing her finger at the top of his head. Walt explained that he was never more embarrassed in his life than he was as he trudged up the steps. It was the longest walk of his life, with 23,000 fans watching him. Fortunately, he was able to convince the usher as to what actually had happened and was allowed to return to his seat. He was rather calm for the remainder of the game.

Every starter returned for the 1979-80 year, along with two more All-American recruits, Greg Kite from Houston, Texas; and Mike Maxwell from Highland High school in Salt Lake City. The foundation had been laid. We were solid from top to bottom. The future would indeed be bright.

The first road trip of the year provided us with a couple of heart-stoppers that aged me twenty years. We traveled to Tulsa, Oklahoma to play Tulsa University and Oral Roberts University.

I felt we were a superior team to Tulsa but played so poorly we found ourselves trailing most of the second half. With 5:36 remaining in the game, Tulsa led 67-60. At that point, Greg Ballif, Fred Roberts, and Dan Ainge went to work. Greg hit a jump shot from the side, Fred drove for a layup, Greg hit another jump shot followed by a fourth consecutive goal by Dan. In exactly 2 minutes we took the lead 68-67. We traded baskets and after a couple of fouls the score was tied 71-71 with 18 seconds to play. We called our fifth and final timeout.

Greg Ballif (left) drives against Wyoming as Dan Ainge gets clobbered!

Devin Durrant had been struggling during the game and was not in the lineup the last few minutes of play. I had great confidence in his ability to play under pressure, however, and substituted him back into the game. Devin was an exceptional passer, so we diagrammed a play that was designed to have him pass the ball to Dan for a last second shot. The players executed the play perfectly, but as Dan took the jump shot, a Tulsa player made a great defensive recovery and blocked the shot out of bounds. Two seconds to play—BYU's ball under our basket—no timeouts remaining. Fred Roberts took the ball out of bounds as the two teams lined up for the final effort. Fred inbounded the ball to Dan who was immediately double-teamed by Devin's man. Dan made a great pass to Devin, and he went up for an 18-foot jump shot that hit nothing but the bottom of the net. We won 73-71. I kissed Devin's sweaty cheek as we swarmed the floor in jubilation.

Devin Durrant gets a jump shot off in our 76-62 win over Purdue.

The next night we were to play a much better Oral Roberts University team at the Mabee Center on the ORU campus. Over the years ORU had lost very few games at home. We would certainly have to play much better if we expected to win. The game was to be televised live back to Utah.

Oral Roberts started the game in a 2-3 zone defense. When we attack a 2-3 zone, we normally have a 1-3-1 offensive alignment with a point guard, two wing men, high and low post men. The strategy is to have our point guard, Scott Runia, dribble into the gap between the opponents two front defenders, make someone commit to cover him, and then pass off to either Dan or Devin on the wings. If Dan, for example, were to receive the pass, he would usually have an open 18 foot jumpshot. The only defensive man that could cover him would have to leave one of our two post men (Alan Taylor or Fred Roberts) open momentarily. If that happened, Dan would simply pass the ball to that open man who would, in turn, look for a quick shot from either the high or the low post area. Over the years this attack has been very good to us.

Scott Runia penetrates the zone.

The ORU players were so quick, however, that our players began to hurry their passes and shots. The defense covered the internal passes to our post men so well that our players started taking hurried, long range jump shots. As can be expected when players fall into this trap, we were shooting a very poor percentage. When a shot that is taken from long range misses, chances are very good that the ball will rebound a long way from the hoop as well. Such was the case with virtually every one of our missed long shots.

The long rebounds enabled the two ORU guards to get a jump on their fast break. Our point guard was often the only man back to defend two and sometimes three ORU players. Within a few short minutes, we trailed by sixteen points. It was obvious that our normal zone attack would not suffice against such an outstanding defense.

We called a time out and made a change in our offense. Seldom would we consider making such a spur of the moment change in strategy without having practiced it. It was so early in the season that we simply had not covered all of the offensive adjustments we would eventually employ. Such an adjustment was necessary or ORU would blow us out of town.

We inserted Steve Craig who possessed super athletic skills into the lineup to give us more quickness. We changed to a 2-1-2 offensive alignment with Scott and Steve out front. They were instructed to penetrate the zone with a dribble wherever possible and hit the open man with the pass. Their main responsibility, however, was to make sure they were *both* back on defense whenever we took a shot. We had to stop their fast break.

Alan and Fred were each stationed at a low post, one on each side of the keyhole. They were to work as partners, flashing high and low looking for passes from the other players and then for each other respectively.

Dan was positioned at the high post with instructions to "free-lance," to find openings in the defense wherever and whenever he could, and flash into those openings looking for passes from his teammates. He was allowed to go any place on the court he felt he could get open. He was the "star" in our so called "star attack."

These adjustments had to be given to our team in less than 60 seconds during the time out. Fortunately, they were simple adjustments. Our two front men neutralized the ORU fast break. We slowly began to chip away at the lead. By halftime we had cut the sixteen point deficit to ten as we trailed 41-31.

Steve Craig (left) gets and easy one, and a driving Fred Roberts could use a haircut!

During the intermission, we were able to discuss our adjustments in more depth. Although we had never used nor practiced the "star attack" before, it seemed to be working. We started the second half with a strong sense of confidence. We played well and continued to narrow the margin. We tied the score eleven minutes into the second half. With about six minutes to play, Alan, who had already scored 22 points, was whistled for his fifth foul. Shortly thereafter, Steve Craig followed with his fifth. Steve protested with "You've got to be kidding!" for which he was promptly assessed a technical foul. Just a few minutes prior to that, I had been charged with a "T" for a similar mild statement. I felt that neither technical was justified. It appeared to me that we were beginning to get some good old fashion "southern hospitality" so as the official approached the bench, I asked him, "You're not going to let us win this game, are you?"

"No, sir, I'm not!" was his simple reply.

I muttered to myself, "There's no way you're going to stop us," as I walked away in disgust.

Steve Trumbo replaced Alan and responded with five field goals in seven attempts. Greg Ballif replaced Steve Craig and delivered five valuable assists. The last several minutes of the game we exchanged leads. Late in the game, Dan Ainge went on a rampage. Everytime the Titans would score, Dan responded with two points of his own. He scored our last fourteen points.

With less than one minute to play, Dan scored to give us a 74-73 lead. Oral Roberts called time out. I assumed their coach would diagram a special play in an attempt to regain the lead. To counter, we decided to change our defense to a 1-3-1 zone. Our plan was to plug up the middle and force them to take an outside shot. Our strategy seemed to work, for when ORU went on the attack, their players were confused by our new defensive alignment. They wasted valuable seconds as they scrapped their pre-arranged play. The shot they finally made was exactly what we wanted—a 20-foot fade away from deep in the corner with about ten seconds to play.

SWISH—ORU 75   BYU 74

Our players quickly advanced the ball to mid-court and called timeout. There were six seconds left to play. Now it was our turn to diagram the special last second play. Not wanting to fall into the same trap as ORU, I designed a play for Dan to take the last shot that would work against a M/M or zone defense. We were to swing the ball to the left side of the court to get the defense to flow with the ball. Dan was to cut diagonally across the floor from left to right and come back out on the right wing. Fred was to set a screen on Dan's man if they followed him man to man, or on the corner man if they were in a zone.

The play worked to perfection. The ball went to the left and then back to Scott on the point, he took one dribble and hit Dan with a pass as he came off of Fred's screen. Dan went up with a twenty foot jump shot directly in front of our bench. As he released the ball, I thought it was off to the left. I'm sure the ball curved to the right while in flight and dropped through with one second on the clock. We had the lead once again, 76-75. Oral Roberts was able to call a timeout, however, with one second remaining. I inserted a 6 foot 11 inch freshman center, Greg Kite, to harass their in-bounds pass. They got off a final shot

Alan Taylor was never accused of being timid.

Steve Trumbo gathers for one of his patented slam dunks.

Greg Kite, all 6 foot 11 inches, 260 pounds of him.

from half court that hit the back of the rim. We had won our second game in two nights with a last second shot. Dan also got a kiss on his sweaty cheek.

We have had some particularly special experiences with our players at Brigham Young University. Whenever we play, especially during our December non-conference games, we have an unusually large following of fans. They normally consist of BYU alumni, members of the LDS church, missionaries and investigators of the church. More often than not, we are asked and are pleased to present a special fireside for these wonderful people either the night before the game or following the game. Player participation at these firesides is strictly voluntary. On many occasions, both Mormon and non-Mormon players alike speak. They simply bear their testimony or say what is in their heart.

At the conclusion of our come from behind victory at Oral Roberts University, our players showered and dressed at which time we adjourned to an auxiliary gym also located in the Mabee Center. Awaiting us were nearly one thousand followers who had attended the game.

As the people sat on the gymnasium floor, I introduced four or five of our players. Each spoke briefly about how athletics had influenced their lives and then bore their testimony as to the truthfulness of the Gospel of Jesus Christ. It was a choice experience.

We had a similar yet different experience in Bloomington, Minnesota at the conclusion of the 1978 Pillsbury Classic near Minneapolis—St. Paul. We delayed our departure Sunday morning until after we had the opportunity of presenting a special early morning tri-stake fireside of the LDS youth in that area. The stake center was packed as each of our players took about five minutes to speak and bear their testimonies. It is a time like this that one can really sense the special spirit and the closeness that our players have for each other.

In 1976 we had an occasion to offer a fireside on the University of North Carolina campus. It was during the Christmas holiday and they expected only 30 or so people to show up. When we arrived, however, we were greeted by nearly 300. I spoke for a half an hour and then several of our players voluntarily stood and spoke to the group.

We have held similar firesides at a Church stake center in Norfolk, Virginia; at our hotel in Reno, Nevada; in the heart of Texas Arena in Waco, Texas; at the LDS Institute on the University of Illinois campus in Champaign, Illinois; and many more. Each year we hold a special Courtside-Fireside at the Marriott Center prior to our varsity preview intrasquad game. We have in excess of 10,000 young boys and girls and their advisors in attendance. In addition, our players average three or four personal speaking engagements per week during the school year. They vary from church meetings to school assemblies to basketball clinics.

It has been during these firesides, etc., that I have learned to have a particularly deep understanding, appreciation, and love of our players. I have heard Fred Roberts speak of his enormous love and respect for his parents for teaching him the values of honesty, integrity, and hard work, and the principles of the Gospel. The Roberts boys have learned their lessons well for I have never coached more dedicated, hard working young men.

I have heard Dave McGuire during his freshman year and, as a non-member of the LDS church, speak at a courtside fireside in front of several thousand Mormon youth about the lessons he learned during his youth about the perils of smoking, drugs, and drinking alcoholic beverages. He spoke of care and concern for other people, and true and lasting friendships. His comments personify his personality and character.

I have heard Scott Runia talk of his love for his parents and his desire to live his life by the example that they have set for him. One Sunday evening Scott drove 85 miles through an intense winter snow storm to deliver an autographed picture of him and his teammates to a boy in Ogden named Jason on his eighth birthday. Scott could easily have mailed the picture, but as was typical of his nature, he went the extra mile to befriend a perfect stranger.

I have heard Steve Trumbo tell how every Sunday morning, regardless of how little sleep or how tired they were after returning from trips Saturday night, his father would get each of his boys out of bed and accompany them to their priesthood meeting. The example Dale Trumbo set for his family had an everlasting affect (Dale and Jo Trumbo are the proud parents of twelve adopted children).

Dale and Jo Trumbo and their twelve children.

I have heard Dan Ainge tell of how his father always taught him to live a balanced life. When Dan was young he explained to his father, Don, that he did live a balanced life—he played football, basketball, baseball, golf, etc. He was soon to learn and has since shared with many others, that balance means not only athletic skills, but educational, emotional, social, and spiritual growth as well.

I have heard Devin Durrant speak of how he considered his father to be his "best friend" and how he hoped some day to repay his mom and dad and brothers and sisters for all they have done for him. As well as Devin played for us, his finest hour did not occur on the basketball floor, but rather on regional TV during an interview after we had just clinched our second consecutive conference championship at Laramie, Wyoming. Devin "told the world" how all his life he had been blessed with great opportunities and good fortune. Now he wanted in some small way to repay his "debt" by serving the Lord on a two-year mission for the LDS church. He wanted to GIVE for a change, rather than receive.

In addition to Devin, we have had Stu Walkenhorst, Steve Craig, Craig Christensen, Greg Anderson, Kevin Nielsen, and Mike May serve two-year missions.

Mike May and Alan Taylor were two young men that expressed to us during the recruitment process that they wanted nothing to do with "religion" during their college experience. Within a year or so, their lives were so touched by the environment in which they lived, that they investigated the teaching of the LDS faith and were subsequently baptized. Vern Thompson, Paul Vos, Dave McGuire, and Steve Anderson were likewise converted as was one of our managers, Leonard Welsh and a secretary Debbie Lowry.

We have made a concerted effort to not force the LDS teachings upon our non-LDS players nor to hassle them about it. Each conversion was a result of the individual's sincere desire to study the church—a subsequent testimony—and their request to be baptized. Obviously, not all of our non-LDS players chose to investigate the LDS faith. That certainly does not detract from our sincere love and affection for them as well. We respect their beliefs and honor their right to worship as they choose. We feel we are all better people for having the opportunity to share our lives with one another.

One of the most exciting and interesting strategic games that I have coached occurred at the University of Utah in February 1980. We had won the first game against the Utes earlier that year in Provo quite handily. For the second year in a row the second game against Utah could result in a tie for the conference lead if they were to win, or a two-game lead if we won. That, plus the fact that the BYU-Utah game is easily one of the greatest rivalries in America, made the game a super-charged, highly emotional affair.

The Utah Special Events Center seats 15,000, and it was jammed to the rafters. Our fans were allotted 300 tickets in the upper balcony, but they were there in force.

The Salt Lake Area Chevrolet Dealers had united in their support for the U of U athletic program and collectively purchased well over 10,000 red and white pom-poms for the Ute partisans. As they entered the arena, each fan was provided a pom-pom free of charge. During our pre-game warmup, there was no sign of their existence. We retired to the dressing room for our final instructions, and then took the floor once again for the introduction of players. Our 300 fans greeted us with great exuberance. The Utah team then emerged from their dressing room. Spontaneously, 14,700 fans rose to their feet to the tune of the Ute fight song and began to shake their pom-poms with determined vigor. My thoughts quickly turned to the concern that such an impressive display of colorful support might intimidate my team.

The pom-poms were quickly stilled, however, as we steadily and with precise execution, pulled to a seventeen point lead. Within minutes, however, our three leading scorers, Dan Ainge, Devin Durrant, and Fred Roberts each had collected three personal fouls and had to be withdrawn from the game. With eight minutes to play in the first half, all three were on the bench. Utah slowly whittled away at our secondary lineup. The pom-poms slowly came back to life. Utah hit a desperation shot at the buzzer to draw within seven points at half time. The crowd once again was on its feet.

We inserted our starting lineup as the second half got under way. Within three minutes all three of the same players each had collected his fourth personal foul. The margin had been cut to four points. I pulled Dan and Fred, leaving Devin in the game in hopes he could maintain some fire power and stability. Within sixty seconds he fouled out. There were sixteen minutes left to play, and we were in serious trouble. The arena was one big red and white oval of jubilation.

With Dan and Fred on the bench, and Devin out of the game, Utah crept to a three-point lead only to have us quickly regain it and go ahead by one. There were thirteen minutes remaining. At this point we had to make a critical decision. Having regained the lead, I decided to insert Dan and Fred back into the lineup. We changed to a three guard offense with instructions to go into a four-corner attack game. Within minutes we scored several layups and regained a comfortable lead of seven or nine points. The pom-poms were stilled once again. But Utah was not about to fold. They gamely fought back. We were not to be denied the win, however, and nursed the clock and the score down to a one-point victory: 83-82. It was one of the most satisfying wins I have ever enjoyed as a coach. It was an outstanding and gutsy performance by our players. It had come under great odds with the Utah home crowd at its finest.

We went on to the conference championship for the second consecutive year. We were to be the first team in the history of the Western Athletic Conference to win every road game. Our final record of 24 wins and 5 losses, plus an additional win over the USSR National Team was the best win-loss record in the 64 year history of BYU basketball. It was a credit to an outstanding group of young men, super assistant coaches, Harry Anderson and Roger Reid, and a part-time assistant Jake Conklin.

A Wyoming "cowboy" helps support Devin as he cuts down the nets after our second consecutive WAC championship.

8

FOREIGN TRAVEL

My first and latest trip abroad, as well as everything in between, have been as a direct result of my life in basketball. Without my affiliations with this great sport, I probably would not have ventured past the Utah and Idaho borders.

I first set foot on foreign soil during my junior year at Idaho State College, when our basketball team participated in the Queen City Tournament in Buffalo, New York. Our tournament hosts took the team to Niagara Falls. When we visited the falls on the Canadian side, I recall telling Duke Wiseman how grateful I was for this opportunity, because I was quite confident that I would never be able to see the falls again—certainly not at my own expense.

I was wrong, and yet I was right. Almost twenty years to the day I returned to Niagara Falls, this time as the head coach at BYU. I now have had the privilege of visiting this spectacular area twice in my lifetime, both as a result of basketball trips.

My first real trip abroad came several years later while I was assisting at UCLA. Antonio Diaz Miguel, the head coach of the Spanish Olympic team has visited us on several occasions at UCLA. In the summer of 1973 he invited me to visit Spain to conduct clinics for approximately a dozen Spanish coaches as well as to direct practice sessions for twenty-four young Spanish players. The clinics were to be conducted for two weeks each in Malaga, a coastal town on the Mediterranean Sea and La Coruna on the Atlantic seaboard. They had agreed to pay me a very handsome fee, from which I would take care of all my expenses.

With some quick arithmetic my wife and I decided we could take her and four of our five children (we chose to leave our 1 year old daughter Kali with her Aunt) for the entire five weeks and still have a few pennies to spare.

In July of 1973, my wife, three daughters, Kelly, Kris, and Kipp, our son Gib and I departed from Los Angeles International Airport for Madrid, Spain. Five weeks later we returned to LA after a most enjoyable and rewarding experience.

Three years later when I was the head coach at BYU, Antonio Diaz Miguel invited me to Spain again. This time I would travel to Vigo, Spain during July 1976 to conduct clinics for thirty-six Spanish coaches and coach the Spanish Sub-24 All-Star team (players between 19-24 years of age). At the end of the two-week clinic we would enter the team in an international tournament consisting of another Spanish National JR team (under 17), a U.S. All-Star team from Kentucky, and the Yugoslavian National Junior Team.

In May, six weeks prior to my departure for Spain, I received a telephone call about 5:30 a.m. from Kresimir Cosic from Ljubljana, Yugoslavia. Kresimir was a former BYU All-American who was a Yugoslavian citizen and national hero in their basketball circles. Today, he is a legend both in Yugoslavia and in Provo, Utah. He had a flair for the game that captivated the audiences worldwide. It was indeed a sight to behold this skinny 6 foot 11 inch Croatian dribbling the ball chest high as he led the fast break down the middle lane.

In Yugoslavia, all males are required to spend one year in the army at age 21 or 29. Kresimir was deferred at age 21 because he was in America going to college. When he turned 29 therefore, he entered the military for his mandatory 12 month active duty term. When he called me he had served 11 months but had one month remaining. That created a problem for him, because he had also been hired to coach the club team Olimpia in Ljubljana. Summer practices were to start the last week in May, and he still had the month to serve in the army. Thus, the call to me.

He asked if I could fly to Ljubjana by the end of the week and coach his team for him until his discharge. His club would pay all expenses for my wife and me, plus an honorarium for coaching the team. My schedule was such that I could afford three weeks. Bee and I were able to have all of our children looked after except our son Gibson. Therefore, we decided to take him with us and take the opportunity to travel to Yugoslavia.

Our pre-conceived impressions of the communist country were only partially accurate. It took us at least an hour to clear customs in Ljubljana. The customs officers were very cold and suspicious in nature. We were really given a third degree as to why we were visiting. After clearing, we were met by Kresimir's assistant coach, Debo. He was to act as our interpreter and host. As we became better acquainted, we inquired as to why he had not joined the communist party like so many of the players on the team. He confided to us that he believed the Party had killed his father several years previously and that he would never join, regardless of the lack of advancement and opportunity that it would inevitably bring about.

The president of the Slovenian Basketball Federation (Slovenia was the area of Yugoslavia in which Ljubljana is located—much like a state in America) was our official host. His name was Boris Kristancic. He was a very high-ranking official of the Communist Party. One day as Bee and I visited casually with him, he confessed that communism in Yugoslavia was unlike Russian communism. He stated that they themselves were fearful of Russian communism. He also confessed that it was extremely important to them that Bee and I as capitalists left his country with a very good impression of them. As the weeks progressed it was evident that his group would see to it that we walked away impressed.

I found that the Yugoslavians are a very easy-going (unorganized is a better word for it) group of people. My coaching responsibilities were to consist of two practices per day. More often than not a few of the players (who were paid to play) would walk in quite late or never show up at all. When they were there, all they wanted to do was scrimmage. They were not accustomed to practices as we know them, with fundamental drills, etc. Normal practices for them would usually consist of an hour or two of shooting and horsing around in the morning and a couple of hours of scrimmage in the afternoon.

Club Olimpia of Ljubljana and our host team prior to a game on their outdoor court. Debo is on my left.

The players' ages ranged from 17 to 32. Most of the players were in their mid-twenties and most were members of the Communist Party. We made particularly good friends with a guard named Josip. He told us only ten or fifteen percent of the Yugoslavians were members of the Party. He joined because it would enhance his opportunities to progress in his chosen field much more readily.

At the end of the first week of practice Kresimir talked Boris into flying my family and me to the resort capital of Yugoslavia for the weekend. It is the city of Dubrovnik, located in the south central coast of the country on the Adriatic Sea. It is an ancient city steeped in history and beauty.

After two days of sightseeing and swimming in the Adriatic Sea at Dubrovnik we returned to Ljubjana. Kresimir had made arrangements for us to meet him in Zagreb for two days on our return trip to Ljubljana. He was stationed there for the last month of his army tour. The Club Olimpia was to meet us there to play a game against a local team Monday night.

At the game I met a young man playing for the Zagreb team that I had met a year previously in Provo. We had played the Yugoslavian National Team in November at BYU, and he was a member of that team. His name was Mihovil Nakic (we called him Nick), a handsome young man who stood 6 ft 8 in and possessed what I considered great basketball potential. He spoke fluent English, so we had a chance to visit both in Provo and again in Zagreb. On both occasions he indicated to me how impressed he was with BYU. Of course, Kresimir had played at BYU, and at that time we had a second Yugoslavian, Misho Ostarcevic playing for us.

The recruiting wheels began to turn in my mind. The Yugoslavian people are very sensitive about their players going to America, so I didn't feel it would be wise to openly recruit Nick while I was their guest. I chose, therefore, to ask one of the Club Olimpia players, "Goran", who was a close personal friend of Nick's, to talk to him behind the scenes and get a feeling of his interest in possibly coming to America to play for BYU.

When we returned to Ljubljana we found that the team had made arrangements to go to a small village near the Yugoslavian, Italian, Austrian borders called Kranska Gora. The Yugoslavian Olympic team of which Kresimir was a member was practicing for the next two weeks in the same village. They would practice in the local school house gymnasium from 10 am to 12 and from 5 to 7 pm. We were to follow them in the same gym from 12 to 2 pm and 7 to 9 pm. Kresimir could also spend a few minutes with us each day.

Only ten members of the team were able to make the trip. Club Olimpia had access to a mini bus that seated only nine plus the driver. I suggested therefore, that Bee, Gib and I take the public bus which left Ljubljana every four hours for the sixty mile drive to Kranska Gora. The cost would be something like $3 per person. Boris, however, would have nothing to do with that plan. Against my protest he called a taxi and piled the three of us plus one of the players named Sasho, into the taxi and pointed us northward. On the way Sasho had the taxi driver take a detour to another village called Bled. In all my life I have never seen a more scenic setting. Bled was a small village nestled in the evergreen-clad mountains on the shore of a beautiful deep blue lake. In the middle of the lake was a very small island on which had been built an old Catholic cathedral. On the east side of the lake was a sheer rocky cliff about 300 feet high. On top of the cliff was a castle that had been built several hundred years ago. Sasho had been instructed by Boris to take us to the castle for lunch. The Slovenian Basketball Federation had recently purchased the castle. Boris later told me that they had plans to convert it into one of the world's greatest sports medicine and research centers. "We must not allow the Russians and East Germans to surpass us in the field of sports science."

We then continued to Kranska Gora. The taxicab bill **surpassed** $100. We checked into the KOMPAS HOTEL, which was without question one of the most ultra modern in which I have ever stayed. The village was located at the base of the Austrian Alps. The setting was absolutely magnificent. When we first considered the trip to Yugoslavia, my impression painted a picture for me of a grey, drab, barren countryside. To date, every place we had visited was one of picturesque beauty. Ljubjana could be compared to Eugene, Oregon; Dubrovnik to San Diego; Zabreb a cross between Denver and Chicago (my least favorite); Bled and Kraska Gora like our most scenic spots in the Pacific Northwest. Yugoslavia was indeed a country of striking beauty.

The Yugoslavian Olympic coach, Mirko Novosel was an old acquaintance of mine. Nevertheless, he would not allow me into his team practices. "There is the possibility that you are an American spy," was his justification. It was a ludicrous reason, but I respected his concerns and stayed away.

One morning Bee, Gib and I were taking the chairlifts to the top of the mountain at the base of which Kranska Gora was located. On the way up the mountain we passed the Olympic team as they went through a daily conditioning program of theirs. Each player had another player of equal size hoisted on his back. He then ran 50 yard wind-sprints up the mountain with his passenger. I chuckled as I saw Kresimir struggling through the ordeal.

We had been in Kranska Gora since Tuesday. On Friday afternoon Kresimir drove a rented European Ford (much like a mustang) to our hotel and gave me the keys. He said it was for us to use for sightseeing for the weekend. He suggested that we drive north to Austria (three miles) and then West to Italy (three miles). We weren't about to pass up the invitation.

Early Saturday morning we headed for Austria. We spent a most enjoyable day seeing the sights of the countryside and the city of Klugenfurt. Sunday we drove to Venice, Italy and toured that most unique and remarkable city. It was an experience we will always cherish.

Monday morning it was back to work, if you dare call coaching ten characters for three to four hours per day work. It was really a paid vacation for our family and the ball players as well.

At the end of the week we returned to Ljubljana. Prior to our departure for the U.S., Boris and the players held a small banquet in our honor. I was seated between Boris and another heavyweight basketball official. Midway through the dinner Nick Nakic's friend, "Goran" came to me and said for all to hear that he had Nick on a long distance call for me to talk to. A few eyes rolled as I excused myself from the table.

Nick was in Zagreb. He and Goran had talked on a couple of occasions since we played them two weeks earlier. Nick was aware that I was leaving the next day and that I wanted to talk to him about BYU. We visited about the possibility of his becoming a student-athlete. The idea intrigued him. There were, however, several problems to be worked out. He would have to leave his new club team and get permission from them and the Yugoslavian Basketball Federation. They did not like their players to leave. Finances and visas were additional problems. At any rate, I told him to think it over and that I would be in touch with him. When I hung up I was quite confident that he would join us by fall.

Upon my return to BYU, I sent him an application for admissions and all the related material. After several other communications throughout the summer, he eventually flew to Provo and registered as a freshman at BYU in the fall of 1976. He lasted less than a year, however, because his Federation put severe pressure on him to return.

Several promises were made to him to entice him back. Once he returned, however, the promises were broken. In 1980 he was a member of the Yugoslavian Olympic team that won the Gold Medal in Moscow.

I was home for just two weeks when I had to leave again. This time it was for the pre-arranged trip to Vigo, Spain. We didn't want to leave our children alone a second time that summer, so this time I made the three-week trip by myself. By then I was weary of traveling and could have done without the trip. Nevertheless it too was a very rewarding experience.

The next major trip abroad I made was to be the most fascinating of all: The Peoples Republic of China. At the NCAA Basketball finals in March 1979, Bill Wall, the executive director of ABAUSA (Amateur Basketball Association of the United States of America) invited me to be an assistant coach of a U.S. All-Star team that was to tour Communist China in April. Gene Bartow, who took the first U.S. team ever to China in 1973 was once again to act as the head coach. This was to be only the second U.S. basketball team in history to visit Red China. Ironically, the initial invitation was extended to UCLA when I was assisting there. However, Coach Wooden and Bill Walton did not want to make the trip, so it was eventually turned down—thus Bartow and a U.S. All-Star team was selected.

John Bach of Penn State University was to go along as the clinician, Ducky Drake of UCLA as trainer, and Tony Daly of L.A. as team physician. Dallas Shirley was our chief of mission. Bill explained that the team still needed two young forwards and told me to select a couple to accompany us.

My two starting forwards at BYU that year were both freshman, Devin Durrant, 6 ft 7 in and Fred Roberts 6 ft 10 in. They were both exceptional young players with virtually identical statistics as freshman on the WAC Conference championship team. They were ideal in my opinion, so I invited them. They readily accepted.

The team and official party met together at the Hilton Hotel at the San Francisco International Airport Wednesday April 14, 1979. We practiced that evening and early the next morning at Stanford University.

That same afternoon we met at the airport. After a quick briefing by a member of the Department of U.S. and China Relations, we boarded a 747 and departed for the Orient. We arrived at the new Tokyo International Airport twelve hours later. We had lost one full day, plus seven hours en route to Japan. We were bussed to the very plush Norita Hotel just a few miles from the airport. That evening we had our last good meal for the next ten days.

Early the next morning we returned to the airport. In the daylight we could see what we hadn't been able to the night before. The airport was heavily guarded with tight security in the form of armed guards, barricades, and barbed wire fences surrounding every road and entrance to the airport. This security had been necessary because when the Japanese built the airport, they took thousands of acres of farm land, and subsequently had to fight off numerous riots and raids by the uprooted farmers in their attempt to take over the airport or shut it down.

The flight from Tokyo to Peking, China, lasted about four hours. We arrived in Peking at 1 p.m. During our descent we could see the barren, gray, bleak-looking environment. The countryside was dotted with little villages and row upon row of housing that looked like barracks. Apparently they were either that or communes that the Chinese farmers lived in. The land had been cultivated, but there was very little greenery.

We were forewarned to take no pictures at the airport whatsoever. For the first time I sensed the uneasiness of being in a communistic environment with limited freedom. It was unlike Yugoslavia. When we touched down and were taxiing to the terminal, we saw hundreds of Chinese workers dressed identically in blue mao jackets and pants doing manual labor. They had very little mechanical means such as trucks or tractors. Oxen-pulled carts were more commonly seen.

At the terminal we were greeted by the Chinese Basketball Delegation. We were introduced to a Mr. Mu who was known in China as Mr. Basketball. He had been educated at Springfield College in Massachusetts.

They took care of our luggage and escorted us into a large hall where we were to be officially welcomed. The Red Army basketball team was there to meet us. They also had another Mr. Mu—7 feet 8 inches, 360 pounds of him. Tea was served, as is the custom in China, and welcoming and acceptance speeches were made. I met a man who was to act as the interpreter at the clinic, Mr. Deng. He spoke perfect English. Six months later I found that he had been educated at Stanford University, but during our trip I discovered that he had fallen upon disfavor by his government. The reason given was that he spoke English so well that they were suspicious that he might be pro-American.

Mr. Mu, the Red Army center with John Bach. Kyle Macy of the University of Kentucky is on the left.

Mr. Deng was a professor of physical education at Peking University. He confided to me one day that he lived in a two-room dormitory on campus for which he paid $3 per month. His salary was $80 per month. To us that sounds incredibly low, but the average worker in China earned only $30 per month. Everyone has a job, even the handicapped. Upon retirement they are paid 80 percent of their salary.

In the last stages of our trip I quizzed one of the coaches what would happen if his superiors were not satisfied with his work. He couldn't understand why I asked. I explained that in America a coach would be fired. That boggled his mind. He explained that he would be a coach for his entire life. The government dictates what jobs the citizens will have. When I pressed him for an answer as to what would happen if his work was unsatisfactory, the only thing he could think of is that the government would send him back to school for more training and then reassign him.

From the airport they escorted us to the Friendship Hotel. We found that bicycles outnumbered cars in China probably 1,000 to 1— possibly higher. We passed housands and thousands of bicyclists on every road trip we took. The drivers of the few buses and cars that they had were incessantly honking their horns. A horn was honked at least every fifteen seconds as they drove the streets literally dodging the pedestrians and bicyclists.

After checking in at the Friendship Hotel (a hotel built many years ago for foreign visitors exclusively), we dressed for a reception with the U.S. Ambassador at the U.S. Embassy. We met with dozens of Chinese and American delegates. The Red Army team was there once again. I was sitting with their center Mr. Mu, when a waiter brought us a silver platter covered with shrimp and hors d'oeuvres. I took a couple. Mr. Mu followed me and cleaned the entire platter off with one swoop of his hand.

The next day we were briefed as to our schedule. We were to spend five days in Peking, play three games, and five days in Shanghai where we would play two more games. Our clinician, Johnny Bach, was scheduled to give clinics eight of the ten days, six hours each day. It was virtually an impossible task for John, so I volunteered to help him. Together we entertained over 900 Chinese coaches in Peking, and 600 in Shanghai. Mr. Deng interpreted for both of us.

The Chinese coaches had come from all over the country, as far away as Tibet and Mongolia. We were astonished to learn that basketball was the number one sport in China. We held the clinics at their basketball pavilions. Once again I was amazed to see the size and quality of the arenas. In Peking one seated 18,000, and the new ultra-modern coliseum in Shanghai seated 15,000.

During the clinics the coaches sat motionless, with the exception of their hands taking notes for three consecutive hours in the morning, and three more in the afternoon. They never took a break. John and I would alternate speaking for either one or one and one-half hour sessions. One time I asked a coach in the front row to stand up so that I could demonstrate and pass to him. Mr. Deng took the next five minutes to explain to his people that such an act was an American custom. Little did I realize that I put the Chinese coach in a position where he might "lose face" if he were to catch the ball improperly or fumble it.

Two days after we arrived we played the Red Army team in front of 18,000 people. Their coach was the same fellow I met in Madrid six years previously when I saw a game between the Real Madrid team of Spain and the Red Army team. We recognized each other and enjoyed a conversation via my interpretur.

The game was televised nationally to 55,000,000 Chinese. We had practiced a grand total of four hours together, none against a zone defense. You guessed it, they zoned. Although we had superior talent, they beat us by one point. We were very suspicious of one particular referee. However, we were on our best behavior.

The next game we played was a local Peking team, and we beat them handily. In between games we had a chance to visit the Forbidden City, the Great Wall of China, and the Ming Tombs. They were unbelievable experiences.

The U.S. All-Star team at the Great Wall of China.

The last day we were in Peking we played the Red Army team a second time. It is, of course, the best team in China by far. This time we were better prepared, but they beat us in a close game once again. After the game I went into the dressing room to congratulate them. When I entered they were being addressed by a uniformed high-ranking army officer. I immediately recognized him: He was the referee of our first game.

On the sixth day we flew to Shanghai. Unlike Peking, which had a population of 9,000,000 and not a single blade of grass in the entire city, Shanghai's population was 12,000,000 and subtropical in climate. It was a far more beautiful city. We checked into the same hotel that President Nixon stayed at during his famous trip to China a few years previously.

During our stay we visited the Emperor's summer palace, a famous Chinese Vaudeville show, and my most favorite place of all, the Children's Palace. Shanghai has nine districts and each district has its own children's palace. It is there where gifted children are selected and sent to school for special training. We saw little children from age six through twelve learning the arts of singing, playing musical instruments, dance, table tennis, painting, marshall arts, etc. Their choir sang for us in English, "Do Re Mi" from *The Sound of Music*. Kyle Macy from the University of Kentucky was a member of our team, so we responded by singing for the children our rendition of "Old Kentucky Home."

Because John and I were conducting clinics while the team and official party had occasion to sightsee locally and shop in the Friendship Store (much like an American department store that was established for foreign visitors only), I had not had the opportunity to do any shopping. Therefore, our hosts made it possible for me to do so by providing a chauffeured car and escort to take me to the Friendship Store. The escort was a young coach who spoke English fairly well. When we got into the car I told him I was not as interested in the Friendship Store as I was in an authentic Chinese shopping district. He was nervous about that request because it was highly unusual for foreigners to shop anywhere but the Friendship store. I gently insisted, so he had the driver take us to the number one department store in Shanghai. It was a six story building larger than any department store I have ever been in in America. They had every consumer good imaginable for sale under one roof. We had been told that the two major commodities in all of China were bicycles and sewing machines.

The entire second floor of the store was stocked with fabric for sale. I was interested in buying some silk for my wife and daughters. When I stopped at the counter the clerk immediately stopped waiting on his Chinese customer and walked directly to me. Within seconds I was surrounded by well over a hundred Chinese shoppers watching every move I made. I felt like some freak in a side show. I purchased several yards of silk at an unbelievably low price and excused myself. The Chinese murmured excitedly as I walked away.

From there we drove to the Friendship Store. I purchased two Cloisonne Vases that are made exclusively in China. I paid $35 each for them. One year later I saw the identical vases in an Oriental shop on Fifth Avenue in New York. They sold for $800—EACH!!

In Shanghai we played two more local teams and beat each by 40 to 50 point spreads. Once again we played in front of a packed house of 15,000 fans. At the last game the Chinese government had as their guests about thirty U.S. Senators and Congressmen and their wives and/or traveling companions.

I feel fortunate that I was able to visit Mainland China when I did. From what I understand it is already becoming a tourist trap. It was still pretty much Virgin territory when we were there. It's a shame it had to change.

In June of 1977, an Italian basketball coach named Alessandro Gamba visited our campus at BYU. I showed him the Marriott Center and became acquainted with him at that time. For the next two years we communicated with each other. On occasion I wrote a technical basketball article for printing in an Italian basketball magazine called *Giganti* for which he writes.

I discussed with him on more than one occasion the possibility of our BYU team traveling to Italy for some summer competition. He was very receptive to the idea and assured me he would do what he could to help.

At the NCAA finals in March of 1979, the Italian National Coach Giancarlo Primo contacted me and extended an invitation for us to bring our team to Rome and conduct clinics for the Italian Coaches Federation and play some exhibition games. They would pay all expenses, airfare, room and board, and even provide sightseeing buses for us during our stay. We accepted immediately.

The same week I contacted the Yugoslavian National Coach, Peter Skansi, who I was also acquainted with. He, too, was at the NCAA finals. I explained to him that we would be in Rome during July and that we would be pleased to continue to Yugoslavia for a few games if his people would pick up the tab from Rome and back, plus our expenses while in Yugoslavia. Within a few weeks he verified such an arrangement and the trip was on.

On June 30, 1979, our ten returning players, assistant coaches Harry Anderson and Roger Reid, Athletic Director Glen Tuckett, and our wives departed for Rome. Sandro Gamba met us at the airport and escorted us to a residential hotel (Fleming) near the site of the 1960 Olympic games. We met with Giancarlo and other officials of the Italian Coaches Federation late that evening to learn of our itinerary. They had us scheduled to conduct two hours of clinic lectures in the morning, plus two hours of lecture in the afternoon, followed by a two hour practice with our players. Between 250 and 300 Italian coaches were to be in attendance at the sessions. Sandro and a coach from Brescia, Italy, Riccardo Sales, were to be the directors of the clinic. The clinic was to be held at the Palace of Sports, a basketball arena with a seating capacity of 5,000 that had been constructed for the 1960 Olympic games. (That was the year the U.S. team played with Jerry West, Oscar Robertson, etc.)

Roger, Harry, and I conducted the clinics in the morning and afternoon while the players and wives had a chance to see the sights of Rome. Unlike the other clinics I had conducted with an interpreter by my side, the Italian had two ladies in a sound-proof booth who took turns interpreting for us simulateously. The 300 coaches each wore ear phones to pick up the interpretation.

We all found time to visit St. Peter's Basilica, the Sistine Chapel with Michelangelo's works, the Piazza di Spangna (Spanish Steps) and Fontana di Trevi (Trevi Fountain).

Early one afternoon we took the team to the Roman Coliseum to have some pictures taken. I was in a walkway of the ruins when I heard a vaguely familiar voice asking one of our players what university we represented. When he learned that we were from BYU, he asked if Frank Arnold was with them. About then I walked around the corner and met face to face with my first assistant coach ever, "Pop" Corn. It had been well over a dozen years since I last saw him. Here we met again at the Roman Coliseum, 6,000 miles from home, once again as a result of basketball.

Later that afternoon the players toured the Circus Maximus and the grounds of the ancient Roman Forum. Unfortunately I had to return to the Palace of Sports for another clinic.

At the end of the week we played an exhibition game against the Italian National Junior Team. They had also been practicing in Rome

Steve Craig, Scott Runia, Alan Taylor, Craig Christensen, Devin Durrant, Steve Trumbo, Greg Ballif and Italian friend at St. Peter's Basilica.

Our 1979-80 BYU Cougars inside the Roman Coliseum.

Bee and I, Diane and Roger Reid at St. Peter's Square.

that week, only at another site. They were the same age as our players, yet not as experienced. We beat them quite handily.

After we confirmed the trip to Yugoslavia with Petar Skansi, Kresimir Cosic got in the act. He was making arrangements for us to play exhibition games in and around his hometown of Zadar. As is typical Kresimir, we were kept in the dark as to who or where we would play. We had agreed that the tickets for our flight from Rome to Split, Yugoslavia, would be waiting for us at our hotel upon our arrival in Rome. We were to depart for Split (Zadar had no airport service) on Sunday. Each day of the week we checked to see if the tickets had arrived. They had not. We tried to contact Kresimir, he was nowhere to be found. We then tried Skansi—no luck. We finally got in touch with the sixteen year old son of the Zadar coach. He spoke English and assured us he would get the word to his dad and to Kresimir to get us the tickets. Our return trip to the U.S. from Rome was not until July 15. Without the tickets to Yugoslavia we would be stuck in Rome with no expense money for an extra week.

On Saturday afternoon we learned that the people in Zadar had made airline reservations for us from Rome to Split. Saturday evening the tickets were wired to us, and we left Sunday after we attended church in Rome.

Split is a town on the Adriatic Sea, halfway between Dubrovnik (the resort capital Bee and I had visited previously) and Zadar. It was about 100 miles from each. Naturally, we were expecting Kresimir or some familiar face to meet us at the airport, but we were greeted only by the typical rude, abrasive Yugoslavian customs agents. It took a good hour to clear, after which we went into the main terminal to meet our hosts. No hosts. No Kresimir, no Petar, no anybody to meet us. "Here we go again," I muttered to myself.

I asked a girl at an information booth if anyone had inquired about us. She knew of no one. I then saw five sightseeing buses lined up outside with two drivers standing by the door of each bus. I knew two Yugoslavian words—Kosarka which means basketball, and Da which means yes. What the heck, I thought. I'll try the bus drivers to see if one is waiting for us.

I went to the first bus driver and said, "Zadar?" He responded with a "NO!"

I went to the second and said, "Zadar?" Again it was a no.

I went to the third and repeated, "Zadar?"

"DA," he replied.

"KOSARKA?" I asked pleadingly.

"DA," he responded a second time.

I whistled to the players and said, "Let's go; I figure this is our best bet."

About five miles up the road the driver turned to me and inquired, "Hotel?"

"You've got to be kidding," I said, realizing he couldn't understand. "You mean to tell me you don't even know what hotel we're going to?" I had no idea either, so together we drove toward Zadar in darkness.

We arrived in Zadar about 11 p.m. The driver drove to his depot and made three or four telephone calls. Nobody knew where we were supposed to stay. I wasn't surprised. Remembering how well the Yugoslavs treated Bee, Gib and me on our previous trip, I suggested to the driver as best I could that he take us to the best hotel in town. Somehow he comprehended what I was trying to say and took us to a magnificent hotel right on the beach.

We walked in at about 11:30 and to my delight we were greeted by a receptionist that spoke perfect English. "Are you Coach Arnold? We've been waiting for you. Better hurry, your dinner is in the restaurant getting cold."

The next morning Kresimir called me at 7 a.m. and asked if we had had an enjoyable trip. I could have strangled him.

We finally were informed who and where we would play. It had changed three times since our initial agreement. We were now scheduled to play the Zadar Club Team on Tuesday and Thursday, then drive to Dubrovnik for a game Friday night, departing from there back to Rome Saturday. We would fly from Rome back to the U.S. Sunday morning. It was to be a hurried week, so we chose to eliminate our practice sessions, just relax, and play the games.

Tuesday prior to our first game with Zadar, Kresimir told me in his heavy broken English accent that we had no chance of winning the game. I told him not to be too sure, because we had a pretty good team.

"Makes no difference, Coach, we have the combination," he smiled.

"What do you mean, 'combination'?" I asked.

"We have the home floor, we have the home crowd, we have the home referees. It will be impossible for you to win." He sounded sure of himself.

I had forewarned our players that we were playing a much more mature, experienced and talented team than we had played in Rome. I further cautioned them that Zadar had the reputation of being one of the most—if not the most—zealous basketball crowds in all of Europe. I was quite confident that Kresimir's comments about the referees would be accurate, but nevertheless, we were ambassadors of our country, our university, and the LDS church, and we must be on our best behavior.

The first call of the game was incredulous. It was quickly apparent that the evening was going to be a long one. The game see-sawed back and forth. The officiating actually wasn't too bad until late in the game. Kresimir was playing for his old home town team, and put on quite a show as he always did. Most of the Zadar players were out of shape and hustled very little. In direct contrast, our BYU players played with a great deal of enthusiasm and intensity. For some strange reason we actually captured the fancy of the Zadar crowd.

Going down the stretch in the first half, the refs made call after call that kept us from taking the lead from Zadar. I was very proud of our players for keeping their cool and couldn't believe how good I was. I was a great actor. I kept biting my tongue and smiling as we kept getting the "business" in a most obvious fashion. It got so bad that the Zadar crowd actually started whistling at a majority of the calls made against us. (Whistling is the European way of booing.) The last two to three minutes of the game the home crowd was cheering for us to win.

We lost 100-98, but it turned out to be a blessing in disguise. As Kresimir and I shook hands after the game, he draped one of his long arms over my shoulder and said with a big grin on his face, "See Coach, I told you that you could not beat the combination."

Wednesday the Zadar Club rented a boat and took our party on a day-long excursion of the islands that dot the Adriatic Sea near Zadar. The water was blue, and the scenery magnificent. Our former player, Misho Ostarevic, who had returned to Yugoslavia, was home in Zadar on leave from his year of active duty in the army. He and his wife, Ankica, were able to join us. It was a long, but most enjoyable day.

On the way back to the Zadar boat dock, we sailed past our beach front hotel. We were a good 200 or 300 yards out to sea. All of a sudden I heard a yell and a splash. I looked up just in time to see another splash, then another. One after the other, every player on our team except two dove from the boat and began to swim ashore to our hotel. It would save them a one-mile walk after we docked. We were so far out to sea I couldn't help but be concerned. I could see the headlines in the paper, "BYU BASKETBALL TEAM DECIMATED WITH THE DROWNING OF EIGHT PLAYERS." Fortunately they all made it.

The Zadar gymnasium seated approximately 6,000 fans. We had about 4,000 for the Tuesday night game. It was such a great game, with the local club winning, that we expected a capacity house for Thursday's game. We were surprised when game time neared to find less than 2,000 in attendance. A couple of LDS missionaries who were serving in Zadar explained to us that the word on the street was that the townspeople were upset at the Zadar coach for playing Kresimir for 40 minutes against our young, immature boys, and that they were further upset with the officiating. They were, therefore, boycotting the game in protest. Strange fans those Yugoslavians.

On a cliff overlooking Dubrovnik.

We had taken several BYU t-shirts with us to give away as gifts during our trip. At game time we had exactly one dozen left. I had each player roll one up and tie it in a knot. As we took the floor for pre-game warmups, we had the players circumscribe the arena, wave to the fans, and then toss the t-shirts to small children that were in attendance. I took the final two and presented them to the referees just prior to tip off.

When the game started, virtually every fan in the house was cheering for us. The first call of the game was once again incredulous— only this time it was in our favor. The atmosphere never changed and we won in a breeze, 105-86. We had made a lot of new friends.

The owner of the Dubrovnik team owned one of the most luxurious hotels in the city. It, too, was right on the Adriatic sea. We were to stay there for our final two days. When we arrived we found that the game had been cancelled. No one was disappointed. Therefore, we spent the next two days lying in the sun, swimming in the sea, and seeing the famous sites of the old walled city of Dubrovnik. It was a great way to finish the trip.

Basketball has indeed been good to me. Without it my family and I would never have been able to visit some of the great places of the world I have mentioned in this chapter. However, I must confess that someday I hope to revisit a few of these places as a tourist and not have to spend six to eight hours per day talking basketball.

9

YOU DON'T GO TO WAR WITHOUT THE SOLDIERS

You don't go to war without soldiers, you don't hold a rodeo without horses, and you don't win basketball games without talented players. Effective recruiting is the lifeblood of any successful major college basketball program. A coach once told me that the secret to longevity in a job is to exist in a world of mediocrity. Win the first game of the year, the last one, and a reasonable number in between and a coach can last forever. Lose too many or win too many, and people who support the program begin to want more or expect too much.

Recruiting, or the lack of it, more often than not will dictate the tenure of a coach. Regardless of how talented a coach he is, how good a teacher he may be, or how brilliant a tactician he has become his job security is usually affected by the talent-level of the players he coaches. Outstanding players have a way of making a coach look like a genius. Coaches who have little or no talent to work with sooner or later have the alumni and athletic department supporters looking in different arenas for a "better" coach.

The moral of the preceeding paragraph is this: If a coach wants to enjoy his job and be around for a while, he had better get into the trenches and get to work. Coaching is fun. Recruiting is work: Long, hard hours of exciting, frustrating, rewarding, exasperating work.

My first touch of recruiting came at Clark College. It was a very low budget, low key affair. Most of the prospects were either local or recommended to us by a four-year school such as the "Magic" Taylor case. I had a chance for the first time to go into a few homes. It was my inauguration to what over the years has affectionately been dubbed, "The #1 speech," the presentation that is made in the home in an effort to capture and interest of a prospect and his parents

The real baptism into the recruiting waters came at the University of Oregon. I had no co-assistant to teach me the ropes. Coach Belko simply turned me loose and said, "Go." I will be forever indebted to him for his confidence in me.

In an earlier chapter I mentioned a group of businessmen we dubbed the "Under-the-Basket Gang." Early in the fall of my first year at Oregon one of them, Myron Bagley, asked me to join him for lunch. He volunteered his service in any way possible in my recruiting ventures. I confessed to him that I really didn't know what direction to take. Together we initiated, and in subsequent days nurtured, a recruiting network that ended up being a very effective system

Each of the members of the "Under-the-Basket Gang," was made head of a recruiting committee. One was in charge of having correspondence sent to the recruits once they were identified. These letters were from people other than athletic department personnel. Another was to meet the recruit at the airport when they arrived for their 48 hour visit. The recruit was taken to lunch, where he would meet the coaches, some players, and other committee members.

A third was in charge of arranging for advertisement of the recruit's visit. His name was placed on the marquee of the restaurant where we first met, at the motel, if he didn't stay in a dorm or fraternity house, and two or three other places around town. NCAA rules no longer permit such advertisement.

Still another committee member procured river boats for the recruit and his hosts to shoot the rapids of the McKenzie river sometime during his stay. We found that trip to be of great interest to some recruits, whereas it scared the devil out of others. At any rate, it was a favorite part of the recruiting weekend for me.

The second night a recruit was on campus we generally had an early evening party for him. A committee head lined up a booster's home for the affair. The host and his wife always invited three or four other couples who were strong supporters of the program, the recruit, three or four of our players, and the coaches. We normally held it at a house where we would swim, play pool, outdoor basketball, or just any activity for the recruit to relax and have a good time. The hosts would always provide the meal at their expense. It would range from hamburgers or barbecued chicken to steaks. One time I recall the host having catered an eight-foot hoagie sandwich. It was easily devoured by the group.

During the era that I coached at Oregon, the NCAA allowed recruits to visit campus a second time if it was paid for solely by a third party. Therefore, we had a committeeman in charge of second trips. He had a group of men who all owned their own private airplanes. We would send the airplane to the recruit's hometown, pick him up, fly him to Eugene for another 48 hours, and then back home. I found this second trip to be an invaluable tool for "landing" a recruit. On occasion we would also use the airplanes to fly the prospect around the Eugene area to give him a bird's-eye view of his potential new residence.

After we signed a prospect, we more often than not provided him with a summer job, either in his hometown or in Eugene. We, therefore had another committee in charge of job procurement.

The system proved to be very effective. We were able to successfully recruit some outstanding basketball players the very first year. Since the program had been way down, we went after quantity as well as quality. We eventually signed seven high school graduates and two junior college transfers. It took a few years, however, for me to learn that there are more important things to consider during the recruiting process than just a prospect's basketball ability: Things like personal character and serious academic interests. To be perfectly honest, I had little concern about the latter two during my rookie year as a recruiter. That is not to say that all of the players we recruited were "problems." Some of them certainly were quality people in all respects. Others of them, however, kept us on our toes.

Five of the players we recruited did not have a high school GPA (Grade Point Average) sufficient enough to allow them to enroll at the U of O upon graduation. In those years we had a rule that would permit a student to enroll if he had twelve hours of junior college credit with a 3.0 GPA. Therefore, we had these five players enroll in summer school at Lane Community College which was also located in Eugene. At the end of the summer each had satisfied the requirement for enrollment and subsequently were admitted and registered for classes at Oregon.

One JC transfer that we signed that year was Billy Gaskins. We also signed Billy's teammate, a young man we'll call Lou, but Lou didn't show up when school started.

Billy and Lou were both outstanding high school players from Washington D.C. They were recruited by several major colleges. Neither Billy nor Lou had sufficient grades to be admitted to the university that they wanted to attend so an assistant coach at that school placed them at a Junior College in the Rocky Mountain area. It was agreed that they would transfer to that University after one year. One day I was having a conversation with the assistant coach at Brigham Young University, Gary Earnest. Gary told me about these two super prospects and half jokingly suggested that I recruit them so BYU wouldn't have to compete against them. I had nothing to lose, so

I took him up on his suggestion and contacted them by phone in their dormitory.

To my surprise, they both expressed dissatisfaction with the transfer arrangement and a desire to consider other universities. They did not, however, want anyone at their JC to know that they were considering other options. At their request we worked out the following arrangement: For the next six months I sent all of my correspondence to them through a friend of mine in Salt Lake City. He, in turn, would transfer it to a plain envelope and mail it to them from his home. When it arrived it had a Salt Lake City post mark on the envelope. If I called and they were not in the dormitory, I would never leave a return call message. When they left town for their campus visit to Eugene, they slipped out and quietly returned without telling anyone where they had been. For six months we were able to recruit them with few people realizing that we were involved.

After their campus visit they made a commitment that they would sign our letter of intent and join us the next year at Oregon. As the official signing date for the letter of intent neared, Billy and Lou expressed concern that the assistant at the other university would arrive at their dormitory near 8 a.m. to have them sign. Therefore, we made an appointment to meet at 7 a.m. in the downtown restaurant. To our knowledge, our competitors were still not aware that we were seriously recruiting them. After breakfast, Billy and Lou both signed our letters of intent. At 8:01 I was in my car on the way out of town. I've often wondered if I passed the other assistant coach on his way in.

Shortly thereafter, that same assistant was appointed the head coach at a northwestern university. Both Billy and Lou told me that he had previously mentioned that he might become the new coach there and suggested that they consider playing for him if he did get the job. Later that summer we received a letter from Lou who, at the time, was back home in Washington D.C. His letter began by telling us how much he enjoyed Eugene, the school, and the coaches. The northwestern university, however, had promised him that they would build their team around him, make him an All-American, and in addition guarantee him $300 a month expense money if he would play for them. At the time, they didn't honor the national letter of intent, so it was not a binding document, as far as they were concerned. Lou further stated that his parents were needy and that he owed it to them to accept the northwestern school's offer. He concluded his letter by stating that he would still come to the U of O if we would provide him with half of what the other school would.

Coach Belko flew back to Washington D.C. to try to convince Lou that he was making a mistake. When he returned, he felt that Lou would still join us in the fall. He was wrong. In September Billy and Lou climbed aboard a jet on the way west for school. When they stopped in Portland to change planes Billy boarded one south for Eugene, and Lou took one heading north. The last time I talked to Lou was on a telephone conversation the next day. He was in a dorm at the northwestern university campus.

One of the most competitive recruiting experiences I had, as well as one of the easiest, both culminated the same weekend in June 1968. During that era the PAC 8 had their prospects sign a conference letter of intent prior to the signing date for the national letter of intent. Many conferences had the same policy. The conference letter simply bound a prospect to the school within that conference, whereas the national letter of intent bound him to one of the 95 percent of the schools in the nation that subscribed to it.

Al Carlson, a 6 ft 11 in center from Garden Grove High School in Orange County, California, signed a conference letter of intent with both Arizona State University of the WAC and the University of Oregon of the PAC-8. The initial signing date for the national letter of intent had passed, so the recruiting battle for Al continued on a daily basis. I was greatly concerned, because ASU assured him his grades were such that he could be admitted directly. If he chose the U of O he would have to have an additional twelve hours of summer school prior to admittance. He was reluctant to attend both sessions of summer school to do that, because he wanted to play in the Orange County All-Star game in late June.

On Tuesday evening I called his high school coach Jim Stephans to get an update on Al's state of mind. His wife answered and explained that Jim was with Al and the ASU coaches, Ned Wulk and' Bruce Haroldson. Bruce was the assistant handling the recruiting effort of Al and a very good friend of mine. I was sick to hear that the ASU coaches were in Al's home wooing him again. I spent a sleepless night. At 7:30 the next morning I was in the office. At 8 a.m. I called our travel agency to inquire about the earliest flight to L.A. The schedule was such that I could be at Garden Grove High School by 1 p.m. that afternoon.

I walked directly to the gym and found Al shooting around in his street clothes with a couple of buddies. It was the last week of school. We exchanged pleasantries for a few minutes, and then I asked him what he and his family were doing that evening. He apologized and explained that they were going to dinner with the ASU coaches again. This was going to be tougher than I anticipated. It looked as though we were entering the final stages of the battle.

"If not Wednesday, then how about Thursday," I inquired. "That would be great," Al responded.

Thursday evening I picked up Al and his parents and took them to a superb restaurant in Anaheim. We had a very enjoyable time. I felt comfortable about how they responded to my Number Four speech. (Numbers 1, 2, and 3 had already been exhausted in previous meetings. Number four was simply a summation of the first three with an occasional joke or two thrown in.)

As I drove them back to their home, I felt that I needed to stay as close to the scene as I could until Al made a commitment one way or the other. I suggested, therefore, that I had some other important things to discuss with them about summer school and asked if they could meet with me again the next evening. Al explained that Friday night was graduation night and that the senior class was having a party that would last quite late into the evening. "How about Saturday night then?" I quickly asked. They apologized and told me that the Arizona State coaches were coming by once more.

I was inwardly upset, because I had to leave Sunday, and by then ASU would have visited with the Carlsons three times to my one. I wanted one last lick, so I proceded to explain what I had planned for the next few days. I had made arrangements for a private plane to pick me up in Anaheim Sunday morning at 11 a.m. We were flying from there to Santa Barbara to pick up a new recruit named Doug Little on our return trip to Eugene. It was my hope that Al would fly with us that same morning for his second visit.

Adolph Rupp was going to be at the University of Oregon Monday to conduct an all-day basketball workshop under the direction of our P.E. Department. If Al was in Eugene Monday, he could register for that workshop and receive two hours of college credit. That would enable him to attend only one session of summer school to gain the additional credits necessary for admission to the university.

Mrs. Carlson then apologized once more for not being able to visit with me Friday or Saturday, but she suggested that I join them Sunday morning at 9 a.m. for breakfast. Perhaps by then they would have a better idea about Al's future.

Friday and Saturday passed very slowly. Sunday morning I was at the Carlson's home promptly at 9 a.m. I was escorted into the kitchen by Mrs. Carlson and seated at the table. At my place setting was a large scrapbook. I opened it and thumbed through page after page of metriculously laid out action photos of Al along with newspaper clippings covering each of his games over a two-year period. As I looked through the book I consistently paid them compliments for how well it was done. When I reached the final page I came upon a very unusual thing: A series of weather reports from the Portland Oregonian covering from November through June of the past year were cut out and stapled together. One after the other for nearly seven months the weather forecasts read: Rain, rain, rain, rain....I looked up in bewilderment at Al and his parents who had all gathered around me. "I don't understand," I said. "What's going on here?" The three of them broke out in laughter—they could no longer hold back their amusement. Al responded, "The Arizona State Coaches gave me that scrap book last night. For the past four days their assistant has been at the local newspaper office and library putting it together. He wanted me to be fully aware of the difference in the weather between Eugene and Phoenix."

I was somewhat disgusted with such a gimmick, but I tried not to show it. Mrs. Carlson turned to the cupboard and picked up a camera. She then asked me if I had a pen. I assured her I did, and then she said, "Good, I would like to take a picture of Al signing your national letter of intent."

Two hours later we were in the private plane on our way to Santa Barbara to pick up Doug Little. I had not met Doug before. As a matter of fact, I had only heard about him a week previously and spoken to him twice on the telephone. I was waiting in the San Francisco airport terminal for a connecting flight to Eugene when a person who recognized me gave me Doug's name. I called him from a pay phone at the airport. Doug expressed an interest in talking to us, so when I had to fly to Orange County I called him and set up the pick up on my return trip.

While Al was attending the Adolph Rupp workshop, we showed Doug around the campus and town. He was so impressed that after only 24 hours he expressed his desire to sign with us. When we flew the two boys back to California, I stopped off in Santa Barbara to meet Doug's mother. She approved of her son's decision, signed the letter also, and I returned to Eugene. We were two for two for the week, but what a contrast in recruiting.

Doug was eventually nicknamed the "Cowboy" by his teammates and had quite an illustrious career at Oregon. After I left for UCLA, Al fell upon some hard times at Oregon and eventually transferred to a smaller school.

In all the years I have been involved in major college recruiting, the most interesting incident that I have personally been involved with occurred late one night in March 1971. As it worked out, it was both a humorous and a tragic evening.

Each recruiting season a recruiter seems to get involved with one particular prospect with whom he really "hit it off." During the 1971 season, one such prospect for me was a young man named Tommy Lipsey. Tom was a senior at Jefferson High School in Los Angeles. He was selected the L.A. City Player of the Year. Tom was 6 feet 7 inches, 210 pounds, and potentially a great college prospect. As we got better and better acquainted during the recruiting process, Tom and I seemed to establish a strong bond between us.

Virtually every major college on the west coast was recruiting Tom aggressively. We made arrangements for him to visit us the second weekend in March. I felt we had a very strong chance to sign Tom, so we were formulating plans for a most impressive weekend. As it worked out, our biggest rival, Oregon State University, invited Tom to visit their campus in Corvallis the first weekend in March, the week prior to his visiting us. That same weekend, we had three other prospects from L.A. on our campus as well. One was Bill Boyd, the son of the USC coach, Bob Boyd.

Saturday after our early evening get-together at an alumni's home, our players took the three recruits for an evening on the town. I visited with the alumnis for another half hour or so then left to spend the rest of the evening with my family. About 11 p.m., my wife and I retired. Shortly before midnight, I was awakened with the ringing of the telephone. I answered, and was greeted with, "Frank, this is Ralph Miller (Head Coach at OSU). I hate to bother you this late at night, but we've got a problem." My immediate reaction to myself was, "Oh, no. Some of our players have gone to Corvallis and gotten into trouble." Such was not the case. Ralph continued, "You know Tommy Lipsey? Well, we are in the emergency ward at the Corvallis Hospital with Tommy, and he won't talk to anyone but you. Would you mind driving to Corvallis right away to help us out? It's pretty serious."

I assured Ralph that I would get there as soon as possible, and then asked him what had happened.

"I can't explain now, but I will as soon as you get here, please hurry."

It took me less than 45 minutes to dress and drive the 50 miles to Corvallis. I hurried into the emergency ward entrance and was greeted with a very tense scene. Tommy was backed into a corner, literally trembling from fright. He was sweating profusely. His eyes were red and glossy. He was holding an unsheathed ballpoint pen in both hands as though it were a weapon with which he was holding off an attacker. Ralph, his two assistants, Jim Anderson and Dave Leach, a couple of his players, and another recruit were all in the room standing in front of Tommy. It reminded me of a wounded mountain lion that had been cornered by a pack of bloodhounds waiting to attack their prey. Ralph and his group, however, were simply trying to calm Tommy and reassure him that he had nothing to be afraid of.

When Tommy saw me, he was noticeably relieved. "Hey Coach, man, you gotta get me outa here quick."

"What on earth is going on here Tommy?"

"Never mind, jest get me outa here. These dudes are trying to mess me up."

"Ralph, can I visit with you a minute?" I inquired as I motioned Ralph toward a quiet corner where he would explain to me what has happened.

"Where ya going?" Tommy interrupted.

"Well Tommy, it's obvious that you aren't in any mood to stay here, so I need to get Coach Miller's permission to take you with me."

"Talk to him right here, right now!" Tommy demanded.

I asked Ralph if he objected to my taking Tommy with me. He felt that under the circumstances it was the only possible solution to the problem they were confronted with. I still had no idea what had caused the ugly situation.

As we filed out of the emergency room toward a dormitory to get Tommy's luggage, one of the OSU assistants, Dave Leach, politely stepped aside to let Tommy and me go ahead of him. Tommy stopped abruptly and ordered Dave to walk in front of him. He continued to hold the ballpoint pen as though it was a weapon while mumbling something about "ain't nobody gonna slip up behind me."

We collected his luggage from the dorm and promptly left in my car for Eugene. By now it was close to 1:30 a.m. As soon as we drove from the confines of the campus, Tommy heaved a big sigh of relief and for the first time relaxed somewhat.

"Tommy, would you please tell me what on earth has been going on?" I pleaded.

"Coach, them dudes drugged me and tried to get me to sign their contract."

"Come on Tommy, I really doubt that..."

"No sir, Coach," he interrupted, "they gave me some LSD at a party and then got me at that hospital and tried to make me sign this piece of paper, and I wouldn't do it."

"Tell me exactly what happened, Tommy, from the very beginning."

"Well, they had this player, Billy Nickleberry, take care of me. Earlier tonight he took me to this party downtown in someone's upstairs apartment. It was just a small room and really crowded with all these dudes drinkin' and carryin' on. They gave me a CEEGAR and asked me if I wanted to smoke it. Well, I never smoked no CEEGAR before, but I didn't wanta be rude, so I took it and lighted up. Well, they put some LSD in it cause pretty soon I started gettin' real sick to my stomach and my head started gettin' all dizzy and goin' around."

"Tommy, that must have just been the reaction from the hot, crowded room and the cigar," I suggested.

"No sir," he insisted, "I ain't never had no ceegar before, but I have had health classes where we studied about dope and my head and stomach got jest like they said it would in those movies they showed us. At any rate, I got real scared when I started gettin' sick and ran downstairs and outside to get away from things. That's all I remember until I woke up in that hospital and this lady in a white dress and Coach Miller were trying to get me to sign that piece of paper. I knew it was their contract though, and wouldn't sign it. Pretty soon everybody got there and kept hassling me, so I told them I wouldn't talk to no one anymore 'cept you. I knew I could trust you and you'd come and help me."

As I sat and listened in amazement to his story, I had to smile inwardly as it was obvious that the poor, scared kid had simply gotten sick on the cigar, must have passed out, and that the nurse was simply trying to get him to sign the admission form to the emergency ward. As we drove I tried to calm him and reassure him that that was probably the case, but he wouldn't have anything to do with that theory.

We arrived in Eugene about 2:30 a.m. I took Tommy to an all-night restaurant to get something to eat and then home with me. We had a small den in my house with a fold-out studio couch that he could sleep on. There was a big hanging light just above the bed. It was about 3:30 a.m. now, and just as Tommy climbed into bed the telephone

Left to right:
Kipp, Kelly,
Kris, Frank,
Bee, Kali, Gib

rang. I said goodnight to Tommy and went to the next room to answer the phone. It was Ralph Miller. "Frank, we've been worrying about you. Is everything O.K.?" I assured him it was, explained what Tommy had told me, and asked what he knew about the events of the evening. He confirmed that Tommy had gone to a party with Billy and had suddenly bolted from the room. When Billy and some of the other fellows went after Tommy, they couldn't locate him. Apparently he passed out somewhere in downtown Corvallis, because some townspeople found him in the streets, rushed him to the hospital, and called Coach Miller. When he regained consciousness, the nurse did, in fact, try to get him to sign an admission slip that Tommy misjudged as the letter of intent.

The next morning I went to Tommy's room to awaken him about 9 a.m. The big light above his head was still glowing brightly. The covers on his bed were all scrambled as though he had tossed and turned all night. I was convinced he had had a sleepless night.

Our three recruits were scheduled to fly to Los Angeles about 2 p.m. that Sunday afternoon. We had made previous arrangements to shoot the rapids of the McKenzie River with them prior to their departure. Since the afternoon flight was the next available flight to L.A., I decided that Tommy may as well make the river trip with our prospects rather than sit at my home all morning and wait. It was a beautiful spring day, and I was hopeful that the freshness of the outdoors might relax him a bit and get his mind off the traumatic experience of the night before.

The trip didn't seem to help. All morning Tommy sat and stared into space. He seemed to be strangely aloof and still frightened. He was obviously relieved when he boarded the airliner for the return trip to Los Angeles.

Monday morning I explained the events of the weekend to Coach Belko and Norv Ritchey. I must confess that the mean streak of my competitive nature was amused when I explained the look on the faces of the Oregon State coaches when a University of Oregon coach had to walk onto their campus at their request and take a premier recruit from their presence. The incident would surely skill OSU's chances of recruiting Tommy and enhance ours considerably. I couldn't wait to have him return to our campus Friday afternoon.

Later that morning I called Tommy's home to check on how he was doing and to reconfirm the travel arrangements to Eugene for the weekend. Mrs. Lipsey answered the telephone. I identified myself and inquired about Tommy's well-being. She explained to me that he was

still somewhat shaken but doing better. I then brought up the arrangements for his official visit to our campus. At that she got very excited
and nervously exclaimed, "Oh no—there ain't no way that my
Tommy's gonna go back to Oregon!"

I quickly reassured her that he had had his problem at Oregon
State and not at Oregon. I told her in so many words that I was the
good guy, the guy in the white hat that went to Tommy's rescue.

"Makes no never mind," she went on, "Tommy told me about
how you and that other coach was talkin' on the telephone about him.
You two schools are in cahoots and my Tommy ain't never gonna set
foot in Oregon again!"

It was all over. We had lost a super recruit through a freak
incident over which we had no control. Tommy ended up signing a
letter of intent with USC. He transferred to Cal State LA, however,
before his freshman year and I believe from there he ended up in a
junior college. It was, indeed, a tragic experience for a fine young man
that was really a series of innocent events from the very beginning.

Each summer during the month of July, I would pack my bags
and take off on a two-week recruiting trip on the west coast. Bee would
always join me and on alternate years we would take our children as
well. We were able to combine a valuable recruiting trip with a family
vacation. I would spend my days with my wife and/or children, and
the evenings watching summer league basketball games. I would
usually start in San Diego and spend three or four days there. During
the 70's, San Diego had one of the best organized high school summer
programs in America. Pepsi-Cola Corporation sponsors all the teams
in the city. They would play as many as twelve games per night, three at
a time at the Balboa gymnasium in Balboa Park.

From San Diego we would work north, spending another three to
four days in Los Angeles watching selected summer leagues and then
up the coast. Before the trip had concluded, we had usually covered the
San Francisco Bay area, Sacramento, and a summer basketball camp
at Squaw Valley.

During the summer of 1967, I met a skinny, red-headed kid with a
broken leg watching his brother play a game at Balboa Park in San
Diego. He was 6 feet 9 inches and just going into the 10th grade at
Helix High School. That same evening I met his older brother and
parents. I was tremendously impressed by their down-to-earth
sincerity and cordiality.

The next summer I met them again. This time the young man was playing, and it was quite evident that he had the potential to be a great one. During the winter, I followed his progress through the San Diego newspapers. By the time he became a senior, every major college on the west coast and several from back east were interested in him. Most of the national attention was directed to a young man from the east coast named Tom McMillin, but I felt this big red head might be the best prospect in America. I was fortunate in that I had known him and his family for nearly three years now, and seemed to have a good relationship with them.

When his season ended, dozens of major college coaches invited him and his parents to have dinner at some expensive restaurant in San Diego in an effort to entice him to their school. The family, however had established some very interesting, although unusual recruiting restrictions. Rather than go to fancy restaurants with numerous coaches, they decided to select no more than four or five schools which they were interested in and invite those coaches to their home for a dinner with their family. I was one of the fortunate few to be invited to dine with them.

When I arrived at the appointed hour on the given evening, I was greeted at the front door by the father and said, "Hello Mr. Walton, it's good to see you again."

"Hi Coach, come on in," he responded as he escorted me into the living room. "Won't you sit down?" he continued. "I'm a bit embarrassed. Bill hasn't arrived yet. He went to Los Angeles to visit Bruce at UCLA over the weekend. (Bruce was his older brother who now was playing football for UCLA) and was supposed to be here a half hour ago. I'm sure he'll be here shortly, so perhaps we can just visit awhile until he gest here."

Mrs. Walton and Bill's younger brother, Andy, joined us. We visited for nearly an hour but Bill still had not arrived. The Waltons were both nervous and upset, but I reassured them not to be concerned on my behalf. We decided that we had better begin dinner without Bill, so we adjourned to the kitchen. Mrs. Walton had prepared a beautiful roast and all the trimmings. The roast was so big it could have fed an entire team a pre-game meal. There were also a half dozen bottles of vitamin pills and food supplement tablets. After the blessing on the food, Mr. Walton served me and put more meat on my plate than I would normally eat in a week. I politely objected, and he explained that his sons all had enormous appetites and that he had simply provided me with a typical serving. I thought to myself that he had better make a pretty good living to afford to feed his kids.

We just started to eat when Bill walked in. He apologized for being late and then explained that rather than take the bus he decided to hitch-hike a ride from LA to San Diego. It simply took him a lot longer than he expected.

After dinner we went back into the living room where we sat together and visited for a few more minutes. I then embarked on the old Number One speech. Bill and his parents seemed to be interested as they listened intently. I was inwardly pleased with the way things were going. I could sense a positive response from the Waltons.

At the conclusion of my explanation of the U of Oregon program, I popped the big question. "Bill, would you like to make a campus visit to Oregon so we can show you in greater depth what it is all about?"

"Nope!" His answer was quick, cold, and unmistakable. Tact was never one of Bill's stronger suits.

I was taken back by the suddenness of his unexpected rejection. His parents were both looking at him inquisitively as I recovered and said, "I must confess, Bill, that your answer surprises me. I was under the impression that you had at least *some* interest in our program."

"Coach, I appreciate your interest in me these past couple of years and what you've told me about the U of O, but I've got to be honest with you. I just don't think I would be happy at Oregon. There is no sense in wasting your time and money any longer."

I explained to Bill at that point that I understood, and although I was disappointed, I nevertheless appreciated his candor. Not knowing what else to do, I asked Mr. Walton for my coat so I could excuse myself for the evening.

Mr. Walton then asked if I would mind staying a bit longer and visit with them some more. There were some questions that they would like to ask me. Of course I was happy to do so.

Bill and Mr. Walton then asked me some advice as to how to deal with the media and other recruiting experiences. The newspaper and radio and TV station were continuously misquoting Bill and publishing rumors that were not accurate. I offered my limited advice.

Mr. Walton then asked what school I would go to if I were in Bill's shoes. I inquired as to this choices. Bill explained that he had narrowed his list to Princeton, Duke, University fo California at Berkeley, and UCLA. When they pressed me for my impressions, I finally said UCLA. Mr. Walton expressed surprise. He said, "Why UCLA? You'll have to play against Bill if he goes there. I thought you would say Princeton or Duke." I confessed that selfishly speaking I wished he would go to the east coast but in all honesty I would have to recommend UCLA.

"Why?" they inquired.

"Four reasons," I responded.

"First—it's a fine academic institution. Bill, you are a good student and need to be challenged academically. Of course, the other three schools you mentioned are also outstanding academically.

"Second—the basketball program is obviously one of the finest in America year in and year out.

"Third—John Wooden. He is an honest, decent human being and a credit to the game of basketball. I would personally like to have a son of mine play for a man like him.

"Fourth—the distance involved. I have always believed that all things being equal, a young man should stay within a day's drive of his home, if possible."

Bill was interested in my reasons, but he seemed to reject more than accept them. He kept talking very positively about CAL Berkeley. He had been genuinely impressed during his campus visit withing conditions and lifestyle there. When I left his home that evening, I was convinced in my own mind that he would end up at CAL.

Of course, he enrolled at UCLA, and the rest is history.

As good fortune would have it, one year later I joined Bill at UCLA. While I was still in Eugene preparing for the move to L.A., Coach Wooden called and asked me to fly to Los Angeles to spend a weekend helping them recruit two recruits from the east during their official campus visit. I did, and our 48 hours went quickly and successfully.

Sunday morning, Gary Cunningham and I were to meet them at the Bel Aire Sands Hotel, where they had been staying with their hosts. From the hotel we were going to drive to the Marina for breakfast and then to the airport for their return trips home. We decided to take two cars to avoid overcrowding the six of us plus luggage. We made plans to meet them at the parking lot of the hotel at 10 a.m.

The Sands actually had two parking areas. One was the lower level garage on the east side, and the other an upper outdoor lot on the west side. Gary and I drove to the west lot. After a short wait, we concluded that they were probably waiting for us at the east lot. As we drove around to double check, we intercepted one of the recruits walking rapidly from the back patio porch of his room toward an awaiting open trunk of the host's car with a large bundle in his arms.

Gary inquisitively asked, "What on earth is he carrying?" Having stayed at the Sands before, I recognized the object and responded in disgust, "He's carrying the bedspread from the hotel, that's what!" He had it rolled up tightly and was obviously trying to steal it.

I got out of the car and quickly walked directly to the recruit. "Bring that bedspread and come with me, young man," I demanded. He was shocked and embarrassed. Without saying a word, he followed me as I marched him into the lobby and had him surrender the bedspread to the receptionist at the front desk along with his apology.

The next day Gary and I reported the incident to Coach Wooden. After some discussion, he decided to drop the recruit, even though he was considered the premier guard on the east coast. I drew the unenviable task of calling him and his mother and telling them of the decision.

Within a few days we received a call from his high school coach. He pleaded for us to reconsider on the grounds that the young man had never done anything like that before in his life. That particular sunday was Mother's Day; and being from a deprived financial situation, he had foolishly elected to take the bedspread home to his mother. Coach Wooden, Gary, and I met again to reconsider the matter. After another lengthy discussion, we decided once again to reject the prospect.

A few days passed before we received another phone call. This time it was from his mother. She, too, pleaded for us to reconsider explaining that her son had never been in trouble before, and that he had always dreamed of attending UCLA. Another meeting resulted in a third rejection.

A week or so passed. Coach Wooden summoned Gary and me to his office. He surprised us by stating that he had decided to accept the young man after all. When quizzed as to why he changed his mind, he explained that Wilt Chamberlain had visited him on the prospect's behalf. Wilt had finally convinced coach that this foolish act was the boy's only blemish. He further explained how the prospect had turned down illegal financial inducements from several universities that were very lucrative because of his strong desire to play for Coach Wooden. That, coupled with the endorsement from his coach and mother, persuaded Wooden to give the young man a second chance. He had a fine career at UCLA without further incident.

Richard Washington was a young man I recruited for a total of four years: Two for the University of Oregon, and two for UCLA. I first met Richard when he was a shy, skinny 6 feet 7 inch kid from Benson High School in Portland, Oregon. The evening I introduced myself to him he was too bashful to look me in the eye.

It was obvious after observing him his freshman year that he, too, had the potential to be a great player. I started a low key recruiting campaign on him immediately. One of the first things I tried to do was get acquainted with his family. Benson High School had won the Oregon State championship his sophomore year. At the conclusion of the tournament, I sent Richard's mother a dozen red roses with a note of congratulations. From then on I was one of her favorites. For two years I subtly pointed out to Richard and his mother the virtues of playing his college ball in the state of Oregon, and at the University of Oregon in particular.

His junior year I received the appointment at UCLA. The first week I was on the Westwood campus I called Mrs. Washington. I explained to her that I had changed jobs and she assured me that she was well aware of my move. I then asked her this question. "Mrs. Washington, you know all those things I've been telling you the last two years about staying near home and attending the University of Oregon."

She responded, "Yes."

"Well, I've been lying to you. Now I'm going to lay it on you straight."

We were good enough friends by then that the statement brought a great laugh, whereupon I started the recruiting process all over again for UCLA.

Coach Wooden was reluctant to recruit Richard extensively because he lived out of state. During his senior year we played at OSU on Thursday, had Friday off, and were scheduled to play U of O on Saturday. Benson High School was scheduled to play Friday night in Portland. Gary and I convinced Coach Wooden to drive with us to Portland to see him play and then meet with him and his mother at their home after the game.

It is a known fact that Wooden seldom ventured to see prospects play except at playoff games at Pauly Pavilion. When we arrived at the game that night it was easy for me to see why. As soon as he walked into the gynmasium, he was beseiged. Before, during, and after the game one person after another sought to visit with him briefly and/or to request his autograph. There was scarcely a moment of privacy for him to enjoy the game.

Richard played well, and it was apparent to Coach Wooden why I had been urging him to offer Richard a grant-in-aid. From that night on we recruited him very earnestly. He, of course, eventually signed with us and played three years at UCLA before turning pro.

Marques Johnson was a local product from Crenshaw High School, who had a desire to play for UCLA since his childhood. He was, however, a question mark in the eyes of some recruiters, as far as a super-star status was concerned. Marques was actually 15-20 pounds overweight in high school, which gave him the appearance of a lack of quickness and stamina.

One afternoon Marques and I were visiting in my office when he shared with me some of his recruiting experiences. He told me that certain coaches were encouraging him not to go to UCLA because "we had so many talented players that he would not have a chance to play." I asked Marques what he tought, and he assured me that he felt he was good enough to play for us. I then offered these thoughts to Marques. "It seems to me those coaches are in effect telling you that you are a second-rate ball player, that you are not good enough to play at a first-rate institution like UCLA, and so you had better go to a second-rate university like theirs if you want to play. We happen to think you are a first-rate player in every respect and want you here at UCLA."

That same afternoon Marques stayed and watched our practice. Afterwards, Coach Wooden, Gary and I walked from Pauly Pavilion across the courtyard to our office building with Marques. On the way, he asked Coach Wooden who all we were recruiting. Coach responded with the names of Richard Washington, Wilbert Olinde, Jimmy Spillane, Gavin Smith, and Marques. He left out a sixth player, but I didn't want to interrupt their conversation at that moment to correct him. Marques subsequently thanked us and left for his home.

As he walked away, I indicated to Coach Wooden that he forgot to mention Cliff Poindexter from Fresno. Coach momentarily showed exasperation with himself for forgetting to mention Cliff, pondered for just a moment, and then said to me, "Better drop him!"

I wasn't sure I heard him correctly, and asked Coach to repeat himself. "You had better drop Cliff as a recruit." "Coach," I stammered, "are you sure you know what you're saying? Cliff is one of the great talents in America. I've been recruiting him since he was a sophomore."

"Frank," he said, "I just gave my word to Marques that we were only recruiting five players. I can't go back on my word to a young man. It would simply be better if we dropped Cliff. I'm sure he'll end up playing for Tarkanian at Long Beach anyway."

My mind flashed back to the lunch I had with Jerry Norman when he said that Wooden would not only be the biggest asset we had in our recruitment for UCLA, but at times a liability as well.

We not only dropped Cliff Poindexter, but during the four years I was Coach Wooden's assistant, he had me discontinue the recruitment of such super players as John Lucas, who ended up having a great career at Maryland; Alvin Adams from Oklahoma; and Lonnie Sheldon, who played at Oregon State. In each case, the players had expressed a very strong interest in UCLA, and each has gone on to make quite a reputation for himself in the NBA.

I literally cried each time Coach Wooden instructed me to reject these players. He had his reasons in each case, however, and who was I to question the man who won ten national championships during his last twelve years of coaching. He must have been doing something right.

The recruitment and subsequent rejections of Lonnie Sheldon is, in itself, an interesting story. Much like Doug Little from Oregon, it seems that every year an unknown prospect crops up late in the recruiting season, a prospect who can really play. Such was the case with Lonnie.

Jerry Long, a UCLA assistant football coach came into my office Friday afternoon in February. It was the same year we were recruiting Marques Johnson and Richard Washington. Jerry explained to me that they had a 6 foot 8 inch, 240 pound defensive end on campus from Bakersfield who also played basketball and track and field. In football, the word was that he had never been knocked off his feet during the last two seasons. In track and field he had thrown the discus over 200 feet and put the shot 68 feet. In other words, he was a great athlete.

Apparently he had indicated to the football staff that he would really like to play basketball in college also. Jerry's purpose for visiting me was to see if I would mind talking to Lonnie about our junior varsity basketball program while he was visiting our campus. I told Jerry I would be happy to do so and suggested that I take Lonnie to breakfast Sunday morning prior to his departure back to Bakersfield.

I met Lonnie at Ships' Coffee Shop in Westwood at 10 a.m. I was extremely impressed by the big, handsome, yet humble young man. He confided in me that as much as he enjoyed football, he liked basketball equally as well. I assured him if he came to UCLA on a football grant-in-aid we would be pleased to allow him to play for our JV squad.

Monday morning Jerry Long came into my office again. He invited me to drive to Bakersfield Tuesday night to see Lonnie play. I had a free evening, so I took him up on the invitation.

Lonnie looked bigger in his basketball shorts than he did in street clothes. He was a real speciman. As the game progressed, I got increasingly excited about him as a basketball player. He not only had great size and strength, but he had the quickness and finesse to go with it. By the end of the game I was convinced that he could be a great college basketball player, as well as a great football player.

After the game, I introduced myself to his coach. He asked me if I could visit privately with him in his office. When we closed the door, he informed me that Lonnie had confided in him before the game that he DID NOT want to play football in college. Instead, he wanted to play only basketball, and that he would really like to do so at UCLA.

To me, that was both good news and bad news. Good because he was a legitimate prospect and wanted to play at UCLA, and bad because Wooden had already limited our recruitment to just five prospects. I told Buzz I would get back to him.

The next day I told Gary and Coach Wooden about him. Coach was very reserved because of his earlier commitment to Marques. I pled my case for the entire week, however, and finally he agreed we should take a second look. The following Tuesday, Gary and I both drove to Bakersfield to see Lonnie's last home game. He didn't shoot as well that night which concerned Gary, but nevertheless, it was obvious that he was a player.

After the game I presented the dilemma to his coach about Coach Wooden's concerns about six signers. He talked to Lonnie about it, and Lonnie went so far as to suggest he redshirt one year to offset the class distinction.

The following day Gary endorsed my recommendation to Coach Wooden that he offer Lonnie a grant-in-aid. J. D. Morgan went so far as to "strongly recommend" to Coach that he invite Lonnie. J. D. said he didn't care if Lonnie didn't play one minute of basketball, he was such a great athlete that he must be a Bruin, regardless of the sport.

Coach Wooden would not make a commitment, however. One week went by, two, three. When the signing date for the national letter of intent arrived, we still had not offered Lonnie a grant. Tired of waiting and satisfied that the Oregon State University was more interested in him than UCLA, he signed with the Beavers. After a couple of highly successful years there, he declared hardship status and signed with the NBA.

The last year I was at UCLA the best high school prospects were Roy Hamilton and Dave Greenwood of Verbum Dei High School, and a 6 foot 9 inch forward-center who attended a high school in the South Bay. During their junior years, I watched each carefully as they blossomed into blue-chip players. Roy and Dave were not only outstanding players, but fine young men as well. I would continue to recruit them their senior year until I accepted the job at BYU, at which time Gene Bartow and his new UCLA staff picked up the recruitment.

The third prospect was possibly the most talented of the three. His character, however, was subject to serious concern. He had gained the reputation as a troublemaker and "head case." He was very simply a bad kid and not the kind of prospect we cared to recruit at UCLA.

It was the spring of his junior year when his coach and I got into a discussion of the problems the player had. The coach confided in me that he felt deep down that the young man was basically a good person. His personal life had been so traumatic that his personality was understandable. His mother had left home a few years earlier. His father remarried and just a few months previously he had left home. That left the boy without his real mother or father. The last couple of months he had been living with his stepmother.

I suggested to the coach that it may do some good if I were to visit with the young man and talk to him cold turkey about his reputation and chances of playing basketball in college. He agreed, so we set a meeting up for the three of us at the coaches' office later that week.

When we met I pulled no punches. I told the young man in no uncertain terms that he had the reputation of being a "horse's rear end," and that no legitimate school would be interested in having him play for them—particularly not UCLA. I qualified my remarks by making it very clear that if he were to straighten out his on-court, as well as off-court conduct (in other words make a 180 degree turnabout) that he could virtually pick his university, UCLA included. His destiny was in his own hands. Everyone would help him in everyway possible, if he would but put forth an honest effort to change. I wished him luck, told him I would be watching him progress carefully, and excused myself.

The next day I had barely stepped foot inside my office when I received a telephone call.

"Basketball office, Coach Arnold speaking."

"You that dude that chewed my boy's #*&!! off yesterday?" a lady replied on the other end.

I was taken back a bit by the bluntness of her remarks, but I recovered to answer, "If you're referring to ... then yes, ma'am, I guess I am."

"Well I'm his stepmother Mable. It's about time somebody told him what a #*&!! he has been. You're my kinda man and I wanta talk to you. You like soul food?"

This lady didn't waste words on idle conversation.

"Well ma'am, I really don't know; I've never tried it."

"You be at my house tomorrow night at 7 p.m. and come hungry. I'm gonna feed you a soul food dinner and we're gonna figure out what to do with that stepson of mine. We'll straighten him out yet."

End of conversation. She hung up as I sat there with the phone in my hand trying to figure out if I really heard what I had just thought I heard.

I decided to visit a couple of coaches and alums earlier that afternoon on my way to the 7:00 appointment. I met a good friend of mine, Frankie Moore at one of the schools where I stopped. Together we decided to drop by to say hello to a couple of fanatic UCLA boosters. They were brothers and owned a Slavic restaurant in San Pedro. They had invited me to be their guest on many occasions, but my schedule had not made it possible.

At 5:30 p.m. we arrived at the restaurant and walked in to pay our respects. They were delighted to see us and immediately invited us to sit down and be their guests for dinner. I politely declined, explaining that I had a 7:00 dinner engagement. They wouldn't take no for an answer, however, and insisted that we sit down. For fear of offending them, we agreed to join them for just a few minutes.

One hour and five courses later I was stuffed. They brought course after course of exotic Slavic servings and insisted that we try "just a little bit" of each. I had no idea what I was eating half of the time. My evening, however, had just begun.

At 6:30 I excused myself and waddled to the car. Frankie just laughed as I bemoaned the fact that I still had to negotiate a soul food dinner.

At 7:00 I was greeted at the door by "Mable". She was a bright, no-nonsense lady that I immediately hit it off with. After a few minutes of get-acquainted talk, Mable, her stepson, and I sat down for my second dinner of the evening. I didn't dare tell her where I had been, nor did I refuse any of her offerings. She had prepared a very spicy friend chicken the likes of which I have never tasted, grits, black-eyes peas, and some other side dishes I was not familiar with. I was so full I was actually in pain as I slowly devoured everything she put in front of me. Never have I been so uncomfortable from eating. After dinner, we talked some more about her stepson. It was obvious that he could have used her type of concern and discipline well before she arrived on the scene. I was convinced when I left their home that evening that the boy had a fighting chance of making a turnabout.

When I got into my car, I quickly unbucked my belt to give me some relief. Didn't help a bit. Finally I unbuttoned and unzipped my pants and sat there groaning like a stuffed pig as I headed home. "This kid had better be worth it," I kept repeating to myself as I drove in pain.

As his senior season progressed we could, in fact, see a drastic change in the young man's personality. There were times when he had momentary relapses, but all in all it was obvious that he was really trying. His stepmother and I stayed in constant communication. It got to the point where I was calling her Mable and she was calling me "Frankie Babes." (That I could have done without.)

Late in the season she called me about 1 p.m. on a Thursday afternoon. She was very excited. "Frankie Babes, you gotta get my boy a job quick."

"That shouldn't be too much of a problem. Why the urgency?"

"This coach...just called me and said he's got a job for my boy and he's coming to town Sunday to offer it to him. I know that if he takes that job he'll feel obligated and maybe go to that school. You gotta get him a job first so I can call...and tell him no need to come to town."

"Let me see what I can do and I'll get right back to you."

Finding a part-time job for a high school senior in February is not the easiest task. Nevertheless, I made several phone calls and as good fortune would have it secured a job for him working in a warehouse just 11 miles from his home at $3.78 an hour. He could ride his motorcycle and work from 4 to 8 p.m. each evening after school. It was an ideal situation.

I called Mable and told her the good news. She would call the coach from the Northern California Bay Area and tell him to stay home. I suggested that I visit her stepson the next day at school and give him the particulars of the job.

I did, and he was overjoyed with the arrangement. We had it worked out so that he could begin work as soon as his season ended.

When I got back to the office I had a message to call Mable. She was very upset because the coach told her that he was coming to town anyway. He had given her some story about the man who was supposed to pick him up at the airport Sunday was at Lake Arrowhead and there was no way he could get in touch with him to cancel the trip. Therefore, he had to come.

Sunday came and the coach took her stepson for a three to four hour period of time. When he returned, he informed his stepmom that he was not going to take the UCLA job. The other school had a better one for him. Seems as if he could work as a night watchman in a glove manufacturing warehouse for around $10 per hour.

From that day on it was all downhill again. His court demeanor reverted back to the old ways. He pulled a knife one day on another player after a game. Word was he never went to work, but within a month he was driving a new van, sporting a fancy new wardrobe.

Within the next month I had accepted the BYU position. Gary and Coach Wooden had both resigned. We turned all the recruiting over to the new coach Gene Bartow and his staff. Gary had agreed to stay on and help them make the transition.

On the day prior to the initial day for signing the letter of intent, I was in the UCLA office gathering up a few personal belongings I had left behind. It was about 11:30 a.m., and Coach Bartow came in and told me that Mable and her stepson had agreed to meet with him at noon. Gene had not met them yet, so he asked me if I would mind staying for a half an hour to introduce everyone. I was happy to do so. 12:00 came, 12:15, 12:30, and still no Mable or stepson. I suggested to Gene that he call Mable to see if there had been a mixup. When he got her on the phone she explained in embarrassment that she had been waiting for her stepson to arrive since 11:00 a.m. She didn't know where he was. I called the school and found that the boy had left with the coach from the Bay Area about 10:30 a.m.

That was the last anyone saw of him for the next three days. When he returned he had signed a letter of intent with the Bay Area school. He played for them a couple of years. As fate would have it, he was also an irritant in their program before he declared hardship and signed with an NBA team.

I was an assistant coach for over ten years working "in the trenches" as a recruiter. The experiences that I have related in this chapter plus numerous others helped me to formulate a philosophy of recruiting and coaching that I took with me to the head coaching ranks. That philosophy went through quite an evolution over the years.

In the beginning at Oregon I considered only one thing when searching for prospects: TALENT. It was eventually evident to me that talent alone neither wins ball games consistently nor helps to build a solid foundation for a program.

The character of a young man is a vital ingredient that must not be overlooked. Without it, a young man will never reach his full potential, nor will he help a team to reach its potential. Mable's stepson is a perfect example. UCLA was better off not having him in the program. The past several years I have rejected several players on the basis of their questionable character alone.

The most important factor of all took me the longest to realize: A young man's serious desire to receive a quality education and graduate from his university. Too many players today consider college a necessary evil prior to playing professional basketball. I read a statistic once that each year over 25,000 high school players receive all-conference, all-region, all-state, all-america, all-this and all-that honors. Of that group of 15 or so end up playing professional basketball for more than a year or two. That leaves approximately 24,985 young men having to make a living in "the real world." They had better be prepared to do so, and that boils down to a legitimate education.

As head coach I now insist that every young man we recruit realize that a quality education must be his top priority if he chooses to play for us at Brigham Young University. As important as basketball is to all of us it still takes a back seat to education. I must hasten to say, however, that it ranks a close second.

1978-79 WAC Champions: Front Row: Nancy Groberg, Jackie Mutin, Steve Craig, Danny Ainge, Danny Frazier, Steve Anderson, Greg Ballif, Craig Christensen, Scott Runia, Jackie Scott, Tracy Williams. Back Row: Head Coach Frank Arnold, Glen Roberts, Steve Trumbo, Alan Taylor, Dave McGuire, Fred Roberts, Kevin Nielsen, Devin Durrant, Keith Rice, Assistant Coach Harry Anderson, Assistant Coach Roger Reid. Season Record: 20-7. All Conference: Ainge, Taylor, Runia.

1979-80 WAC Champions: Front Row: Tracy Williams, Ihab Elsaadi, Mike Maxwell, Craig Christensen, Danny Ainge, Greg Ballif, Steve Craig, Scott Runia, Nancy Groberg, Julie Lewis. Back Row: Assistant Coach Harry Anderson, Head Coach Frank Arnold, Steve Anderson, Steve Trumbo, Alan Taylor, Greg Kite, Fred Roberts, Devin Durrant, Jake Conklin, Assistant Coach Roger Reid, Trainer Rod Kimball. Season Record: 24-4. All Conference: Taylor, Ainge.

10

THE FAN

In my twenty plus years as a professional basketball coach I have had the good fortune of coaching at three high schools, one junior college, and three major colleges. (Each home crowd had its own personality.)

The basketball fan falls into one of four categories: (1) the fanatic, (2) the loyal supporter, (3) the interested spectator, and (4) the critic.

The fanatic is that person who lives and dies with every breath of a basketball program. Regardless of the outcome of the game, he is totally supportive and has a sincere desire to help in any way possible. This particular fan usually consists of 5 or 10 percent of a team following.

The loyal supporter, although not as intimately involved with a program, will also support it—win or lose. He is understanding, compassionate, and supportive the vast majority of the time. He makes up about 50 or 60 percent of the following.

The interested spectator is that fan who "is with a team—win or tie." He is one who enjoys an athletic performance when it is enjoying success. When a team is winning consistantly, he fills the final 20 to 25 percent of the seats. But when a team is floundering, he usually finds some other way to spend his entertainment dollar.

The critic is that fan which all programs can do without. Fortunately, it is usually made up of less than 5 percent of a team following. This fan, of course, will attend the games so he can sit in his misery and "offer his expertise" to anyone within ear shot. Winning the contest usually is not enough to satisfy this "fan." He will normally complain because the margin of the victory was not great enough, that the coach didn't play the right combinations, that the players did not execute properly, that poor decisions were made, etc. Sad, but true, this person's negativism toward athletics is usually mirrored by his personality and daily outlook of life. I'm not talking about the anxious parent. They are another matter entirely. I'm not even talking about the former little league, church league or even high school player or coach who has had limited experience and expresses his "expertise" as the game develops. That's part of the world of sports, and I feel a

"Rise and Shout...

the Cougars are out!"

healthy part of it. And I'm certainly not talking about the average fan who lives and dies with the emotion of the game.

I'm talking about the 1 or 2 percent of the critics who have all the answers all the time—the fan who has absolutely no involvement whatsoever with the exception of the $5 he paid to see the game or his "alumni pride" at stake. It is not important to him that the coach has been studying the game all his adult life and has worked two to three hours daily for weeks and months and years with his players in preparation, and who 99 percent of the time has a very practical, thought-out, experienced reason for making certain decisions.

This is the fan you can never satisfy. This kind of fan is one that will constantly take the "cheap shot" at a player or a coach or even at other fans around him who challenge his stability.

An incident perpetuated by such a critical fan practically destroyed the confidence and effectiveness of one of my players a few years ago. This particular player was a starter, a very intelligent, skilled passer and dribbler, but limited in his shooting ability. His role was to be our team leader, to establish our offense, and to direct our club so that our better shooters would have ample opportunity to score. The other starting guard was a freshman, and our first substitute guard was a freshman.

In one particular home game about half way through the season, our starter (we'll call him John) was having a rough time. It was very simply a bad game for him. I substituted the frosh sub, and he responded with a rather substantial performance. With about two and one-half minutes to go in the first half, however, he committed his third foul. The obvious decision was to replace him for the last two minutes so he wouldn't get his fourth foul. He was playing so well that I had every intention to start the second half with him. John went back into the game and as fate would have it, quickly committed another turnover and missed a shot. The buzzer sounded, and we were walking off the floor toward the tunnel that lead to the dressing room. John was one step ahead of me. Suddenly, a sharp isolated voice from the crowd less than a dozen rows up from the floor cried out, "Get that bum John out of the game, Arnold, you idiot." It was obvious that his wrath was meant for me, but little did he realize that his verbal anger was like a stab in the back for John. I could see John simply wilt with devastating rejection when he heard that statement. Seldom in my professional career have I been so angered by such an asinine attack.

I started the freshman the second half, and he played reasonably well until he fouled out with about eight minutes to play. John was inserted back into the game, and my worst fears were soon confirmed. His first shot was an air ball. His ball handling and passing were unstable. It was quickly and unmistakably clear that he was playing with little or no confidence. He was a shell of himself. He never really recovered during our remaining five home games. Ironically, he continued to play quite well in our away games. What a shame it was that a selfish, unstable critic didn't have the common sense or decency to vent his frustration in a more positive manner.

This same kind of fan is the guy who will write hate mail to coaches; and yes, unfortunately, to players as well. Ninety percent of the time it is anonymous, of course. He normally doesn't have the courage to act or speak in such a manner if he had any inclination that he might be found out or challenged.

Hate mail was a new experience for me. As an assistant coach, I never received such a letter in ten years. The first year I was at BYU, however, I was shocked beyond description when I received my first. It preyed on my mind for days. I had difficulty sleeping. The second and the third and the fourth were no easier. My only solace was that for every negative letter I received, I received at least 20 positive letters in turn. Nevertheless, the bad ones hurt and they hurt a lot.

For two years I read every piece of hate mail that I received. When a person signed his name, I would make every effort to call him and discuss his concerns personally. We usually parted friends, but not always. One "expert" writes me annually and signs his name but never leaves an address and mails the letter from different towns. Courageous person, that man. His fifth annual letter, among other things, accused our coaching staff of not being able to teach our players how to shoot free throws. He was pretty vicious in his comments. One of my assistants recognized the name so we traced down his place of employment. He was a junior high school teacher. I called him. When he answered the telephone I introduced myself and was met with stunned silence on the other end of the line. Finally, he blurted, "Now I know what kind of a person you really are, calling me like this." Talk about an ironic statement. I told him I had received his letter regarding our ineptness in teaching free throws and was curious to know where he had gained his expertise. He explained that he coached little league teams. That, of course, explained it. I suggested, therefore, that he drop by practice sometime during the week and I would give him an hour to work with out team. It was obvious that he could help us and I would appreciate his help. He said he was too busy, and couldn't make it.

After several sleepless nights and more anguish than I felt was necessary, I decided to do what John Wooden's secretary had been doing for years. I would have my secretary screen all my mail and throw the hate mail in the trash can where it belongs. I no longer wanted to read it, let alone even know it had arrived. For the past few years, therefore, I have not seen nor read any. At the conclusion of each year, I have asked my secretary what the volume has been. Although we were fortunate enough to have had a highly successful season recently, I still receive a half dozen or so each year.

One letter that I received in 1978 was addressed:

Head Basketball Coach
Provo, Utah

It was meant for one of my colleagues at another university, but because the mailing address was Provo, Utah, it ended up in my office. When the secretary read it she brought it to me to ask if she should forward it. I felt my friend didn't need that kind of mail any more than I did, so I chose not to send it on. To this day, he has never seen it. It is a typical letter. Since we have thrown away all of my hate mail, I will share this one with the readers. It is my intent simply to share a typical letter and not embarrass anyone.

Sedona, Arizona
March 17, 1977

Dear Coach—

The wife and I were sitting here at home tonight and shortly after the start of the second half I tuned in the game between you and   . For some reason or other, don't ask me why, I was rooting for you. That is until the last few minutes when I saw your men running around like a bunch of chickens with their heads chopped off: it was enough to make me want to puke #*&%!! -.

I'm sure, Sir, that you know a lot about basketball. Otherwise you wouldn't be the coach at_____. I am even more sure that you don't know a %¢&*!#% thing about *defense*. Or if you do you have certainly kept it a secret from your players. The minute the other team went into a semi-stall, you were dead. Why? Because your players knew nothing about guarding a particular man. It appeared that the only thing they knew how to do defensively was play a relatively poor zone defense, and knew absolutely nothing about a man-to-man defense. Result? When your men were hopping around like the beheaded chickens they so aptly mimicked, the other team made several baskets by men who were *wide open* going in to the hoop. Your man was who *supposed* to be guarding the man trailed him by several feet!! If I had played defense like that years ago as an Indiana high school player, I not only wouldn't have made the team, I wouldn't even have made the squad. And that was high school!!

My advice to you, Sir, is to scout around the find the best defensive coach that you can lay your hands on. Then hire him, even if you have to pay part of his wages out of your own pocket. That is if you *really* have a desire to field a first class team year after year at _____ .

Sure, if and when you are lucky enough to have a bunch of good sharpshooters who play a good offensive game you are going to win a lot of ball games. But *you are not going to win the big ones*! Why? Because you are going to be playing another team who also has a bunch of sharpshooters who are good on offense, but who have also been taught what a good defense is, *and how to play it*!!

I felt so strongly about this I had to get it off my chest. Sorry about that. I've never written to anyone like this before, and probably never shall write. I had (and do not have) any particular interest in either team. I just happened to want you to win and was sickened by their feeble, futile, childish efforts in the last few minutes. Things could be better in the future—the ball is in *your* court.

Sincerely,

Parents are a story all their own. I doubt if I am much different than most basketball coaches in that each year I have five sets of parents who think that I am a pretty nice, fairly bright guy, most of the time. But there are usually seven to ten sets of parents who question my intelligence a good portion of the season. That was also very difficult for me to understand and to live with until my only son became old enough to get involved in little league baseball, basketball, etc. It became obvious to me very quickly that those coaches who couldn't see the hidden talents my son possessed weren't "with it" and needed a little help. Fortunately, there were other coaches who recognized his abilities and gave him ample playing time. These men were very obviously better students of the game and needed to be complimented for the keen awareness.

Every emotion that I have witnessed as a coach—joy, sadness, pride, embarrassment, exhilaration, anger, etc., I have also felt as a parent, only in far greater magnitude.

Gib working on his left hand.

If there is one lesson that I have learned since my son started participating in organized sports it is that "It is much harder to be a parent than it is to be a coach." I believe that I have learned patience, tolerance, understanding, far better than ever before. I honestly and sincerely believe that I have become a better coach the last few years as a direct result of being a parent and viewing the players under my jurisdiction from a different perspective—that each player I coach is also a son of some very loving, very caring parents, and that it is my responsibility to treat them with as nearly as possible the same love and concern.

The vast majority of my relationships with parents has been very pleasant indeed. Few people realize that coaches, too, are very human people with feelings and needs like everyone else. For the most part, coaching is not a financially rewarding profession. The real reward is the firm handshake, the arm around your shoulder, the hug, the tear in the eye, the sincere "thank you" from players and from parents. I have certainly had my share of those rewards over the years, and I am eternally grateful for them.

There are obviously some unpleasant experiences as well. Unfortunately, we tend to remember them more vividly than the positive experiences. It hurts when a father avoids you after a game or at an alumni gathering. It hurts when he calls you Coach or Mr. Arnold, when at one time you were on a first-name basis during the recruiting process while everyone was high and full of positive expectation for their son. It particularly hurts when your wife and children have to sit in the stands and hear parents make unkind comments of different degrees.

Not too many years ago I coached a young man who told me he had been promised by the previous head coach during the recruiting process that he would start every game for four years if he were to attend that particular institution. I replaced that coach and inherited this young man as a junior. A year later a disciplinary matter made it necessary to suspend the player for a couple games. At the conclusion of the first game his mother approached my wife, who was accompanied by my eight year old son, and very sternly threatened to "see to it that your husband be fired." That hurts.

The home fan—bless 'em—what would we do without 'em. In my 20 plus years as a professional basketball coach, I have had the good fortune of coaching at three high schools, one junior college, and three major universities. Each home crowd had its own personality.

Payette High School was not really into basketball. Payette (home of Harmon Killebrew) is a baseball town, pure and simple; football and basketball were simply necessary evils until springtime and the bats and balls could be broken out again. Nevertheless, it was a great town, and I enjoyed one initial year there greatly.

Of all the schools in America, Pocatello High School had to be among the top as far as crowd support is concerned. Of particular note was the highly organized and enthusiastic pep club and pep band. Absolutely super. The student body, however, sometimes became too involved.

One weekend we played our traditional rivals at Idaho Falls High School. We had the good fortune of beating them at Idaho Falls by two points. We had the team bus plus seven charter buses full of students in attendance. After the game as we were all loaded on our buses, hundreds of Idaho Falls students and supporters surrounded our buses and began to rock them back and forth. I must admit that although no harm was done, it was somewhat of a scary situation.

A few weeks later we were to play Idaho Falls in Pocatello. Our administration sensed that there might be a problem and prepared to prevent anything serious from happening.

This time Idaho Falls beat us by four points. To avoid an incident, the administration held the Idaho Falls fans in the stands until all the Poky fans had exited. Police surrounded the gym on all four sides and for two blocks dispersed any groups. The IF fans were released. No incidents took place—near the school.

No one realized that a certain group of Poky High trouble makers organized themselves to scatter and meet as a group at the only entrance available at that time to the new freeway between Pocatello and Idaho Falls. When the caravan of IF booster cars arrived at the entrance, they ran into a mini blockade and as one can imagine, more than just a few fights broke out. This incident was certainly the exception rather than the norm, and it must quickly be said that had never occurred before nor after this one isolated occasion.

The fans at Clark College were nothing extraordinary. We had no dormitories on campus, therefore, all of our students were commuters. At first the student support was not strong, but we had the good fortune of recruiting some fine, exciting players like "Magic" Taylor and Matt Jones. Before leaving Clark two years later, most of our crowds were well near capacity (about 1500 or 2000). It was at Clark where my two oldest children, Kelly and Kris, had their first experience as mascot cheerleaders. They were five and three years old at the time.

The fans at the University of Oregon were a breed all their own. I have previously mentioned the tumultuous support in the UO-UCLA game as well as the distasteful experience with the militant BSU group. It must be remembered, however, that that particular group consisted of only 300 people who were not supported nor endorsed by the typical University of Oregon fan.

It is difficult for me to assess the UCLA supporters. In the four years I spent with the Bruins, we never lost a home game. The crowd was great. I never sensed it to be a viscious crowd. And for an opponent, I never felt the Pauly Pavilion was a difficult place in which to play. I felt that same way when I was at the U of O and reconfirmed my feelings during a recent trip to Pauly as the head coach at BYU.

Although the UCLA crowd was not what I call viscious, it was certainly a proud group, a vocal group, even perhaps a sophisticated group. Above all, however, it was a spoiled group. Having won so many games over the years they really had little idea of the realities of the athletic world. After all, 50 percent of all the teams lose, but nobody knew much about that at UCLA. I guess the best possible way to explain a UCLA crowd is to label it a social group. It was, in fact, a social gathering when a UCLA basketball game took place. Attendance of Hollywood stars and starletts was somewhat commonplace. My wife sat directly in front of one of our team physicians, Dr. Rodney Turner, who practices in Pacific Palisades. He would often have a "heavyweight" as his guest. Some of the ones who attended with him most frequently were Joseph Cotton, James Arness (whose presence always excited my young son) and Walter Matthau. Often Matthau was accompanied by his young teenage son who thought he was a radio sportscaster and proceeded to announce the game—much to my wife's chargrin—from beginning to end. I recall seeing Bill Cosby and his beautiful wife quite often. George Foreman walked in late one evening and caused a stir among his fans.

The UCLA students were real loyalists. I recall one Friday night game when I observed a fairly large number of the students bringing sleeping bags with them to the game. Their intent was, of course, to set up camp immediately after the game to sleep overnight in line to assure themselves of good seats to the Saturday night game with Notre Dame.

The doors to the pavilion remained closed and locked until 5:15 the evening of the game. At precisely 5:15, a bell would ring and the ushers would simultaneously open all of the doors to allow the students to enter. Since the seats were on a first come first serve basis, there was inevitably an avalanche of bodies cascading down the stairs in an attempt to secure front row seats. It always amazed me that no one ever seemed to be injured during this mass attack on the seats. By 5:30, the student section was normally filled to capacity.

My favorite face in the crowd belonged to a UCLA professor of mathematics who abandoned his faculty seats to join the students in their weekend offensive. He always managed to get near center court no more than three or four rows up. He was in his early 30's; about 5 feet 8 inches tall; nearly bald-headed, with wild, free swaying strands of long red hair flying from each side of his head; wire-rimmed, round spectacles; faded, well-worn blue jeans with suspenders and a crazy tee-shirt. Great guy—great fan!!

Perhaps the most ludicrous statement I recall came from a so-called fan the day after we were beaten by Notre Dame at South Bend. It was our first loss after 88 consecutive victories. This particular "fan" I overheard saying to another in reference to Coach Wooden, "Well, I guess the old man is over the hill." Had the comment not been so completely asinine I probably would have interrupted the conversation to challenge him.

My experiences as a basketball coach have been many and varied. My family and I have been blessed in that every place we have been, whether it be at the high school, junior college, or major university level, we have met some wonderful people. Our lives have been enriched each year at each school. Our experience at Brigham Young University has, for the most part, been the most rewarding.

Basketball and Brigham Young University are synoymous. It seems as if basketball has been, and I believe always will be, king in the Rocky Mountain areas, particularly in the state of Utah. No state in the union has more fans per capita attending basketball games at the collegiate level than in Utah. The Brigham Young University basketball pavilion, the Marriott Center, has the largest seating capacity of any on-campus arena in America, 22,700 permanent seats. The 1979-80 basketball season was sold out for the season. During one game there were 23,086 fans jammed to the rafters. All this in the small, quiet college town of Provo, Utah. But on Saturday night when BYU is

The Marriott Center—BYU—Largest on-campus basketball arena in the country.

Sold out!! All 22,700 seats.

in town, it is not quiet. The Marriott Center is jumping. The BYU fans take their game seriously. Bobby Knight once told a group of coaches in my presence that the BYU coaching job was one of the three most difficult in the country. His reason was that the Mormon Church has for many years organized and administered the biggest amateur basketball program and tournament in the world. Since virtually all young LDS men have participated in that basketball program, they all tend to think they are "experts" in the game. I had never heard of nor subscribed to that theory before, but after coaching at BYU for a few years and listening to the varied advice that I receive from the fans (usually during and after the game—seldom before), I'm not too sure Bobby wasn't accurate in his assessment.

One of the most humorous incidents that I have ever heard of involving a spectator took place at BYU not too many years ago. I was not coaching at BYU at the time, so unfortunately I did not see the incident. I have heard about it so often from fans who were at the game that it bears repeating.

The Cougars were involved in the usual, hotly contested WAC game. A call was made by the baseline official that met with great displeasure among BYU partisans. Particularly upset was a local attorney in his late 50's, sitting directly behind the official on the front row. In his total exasperation over the call, he threw his arms into the air, sending his overcoat flying in the process. As the story goes, the coat unfolded and gently fluttered downward completely covering the head and shoulders of the official. The crowd went wild! So did the official.

Needless to say, the official had the gentleman ejected from the game. His exodus was cheered with a hero's welcome—err, departure. The story continues that upon his arrival at home his wife, who was not able to accompany him to the game, was obviously surprised to see him arrive home early. She had been listening to the game on the radio and quickly asked him, "Were you still there when that old fool threw his coat over the referee?".....

The BYU crowd, as is every basketball crowd, is made up of community supporters and students. In 1979-80, over 16,200 seasons tickets were sold with the remaining 6,500 seats reserved for students. A particular point of interest to me is that during each game prior to the tip-off I witnessed dozens of elderly couples well over 65 years of age shuffling through the lower corridor from the elevator to their seats. It is little wonder when one observes this why our adult section is never as boisterous as the student section. We have one special lady who works in the administration office on campus who never misses a game—nor a stitch. For years she has sat about six rows behind the visitor's bench and knits during the entire game. That is, she knits scarves, sweaters, and socks during every single minute of every single game and never misses a stitch.

An incident that was not funny at the time, but that we have long since had many good laughs over, occurred in another game against Utah in 1977. We were struggling, as we often did that particular year, and I was being given a pretty good working-over by this one isolated fan behind our bench. I have always tried to tune out fan's comments; but regardless of what anyone says, a coach can hear them, and they hurt. Nevertheless, I have always been able to ignore them and refrain from a confrontation with critics either home or away. We were being beaten badly, however, and my fuse was growing short. After about the third verbal blast, I quickly turned around to see if I could locate my "friend." My eyes immediately fixed on a young man in the first row who had both hands clenched around the stainless steel railing, his face reddening, jugular veins and eyes bulging as he was about to unleash another "suggestion." I beat him to it, however, as I sternly suggested to him to "keep his mouth shut." About that instant I saw a strong, blue-suited arm reach across the woman next to him, grasp this young critic by the arm and say, "Be quiet! Sit back and be quiet!" It was President Oaks, and he was reprimanding his young guest sitting next to his wife. My heart went directly to my throat. I turned quickly around, slumped down in my seat, and whispered to my assistant, "Pack your bags; I think I'm about to get the pink slip."

At the conclusion of the game I wanted to hide, but instead I approached the President to apologize. He, too, was seeking me to apologize. We both had a good laugh. As it turned out, his young guest is, in fact, one of our very best and strongest supporters. He was simply caught up in the emotion of the game and the thrashing that we were taking from our biggest rivals. That's what the crazy game does to the majority of us.

When I was coaching at the University of Oregon I felt that our fans were, as I have previously mentioned, a super group. However, when I moved to UCLA and returned to the U of O for the UCLA-UO games in Eugene, I found that the crowd had taken on a new look. Strange, isn't it, how one's position changes the environment and perspective about him.

I could certainly see upon my return why I enjoyed the home

crowd at U of O while I was coaching there. I assure you the MacArthur court is not an easy place in which to play as a visiting team. The crowd gets "involved."

Wooden taught me a great lesson once on composure and how to deal with over-zealous fans. UCLA had just defeated the U of O at Eugene. As we were leaving the floor the ushers had to rope off a pathway across the corridor that separated the playing floor from the stairs leading down to the dressing room. The rope barriers were lined four deep with irate fans, each in his own way taking a shot at the players, and particularly at Wooden as we walked by. One extremely volatile man made a very abusive comment. Wooden usually ignores such things and continues on his way. In this instance, however, he abruptly made an about face and walked directly to the man, greeting him face to face. Very calmly, and with a gentle smile on his face, Wooden said, "I'm sorry sir, I didn't hear exactly what you said. Would you please repeat yourself for me?" Well, as you can imagine, once confronted, the man was extremely embarrassed and mumbled something to himself as he quickly retreated from the scene. Coach Wooden showed no emotion, said not another word, and continued down the stairs to the dressing room. In his own gentle way, he had demonstrated to this man and all others who witnessed the incident what a fool that fan and others were making of themselves.

Some crowds are obviously more intimidating than others. The beautiful, spacious new arenas cropping up all over America makes the intimidations of the crowd much less of a factor than before. The most difficult place to play continues to be in those arenas that are small and congested with the fans surrounding the floor such as MacArthur court at the U of O. I recall the days when the U of California—Berkeley program was strong and the fans used to pack the old Harmon Gym. The famous straw hat band sat in the bleachers adjacent to the floor. Cal used to apply the full court press, and the band always helped the referee with the 10 second backcourt count. The bass drummer would beat every count as the band members in unison would chant "one-two-three-four," etc. The only problem was that the cadence would invariably quicken so that a full ten second would be covered in about seven or eight. Subconsciously the ref's hand would start pumping faster with the cadence, the dribbler would hurry unnaturally, and a lot of turnovers were committed.

The "Pit" at the University of New Mexico in Albuquerque has made quite a reputation for itself as a tough place to play. Its reputation is well-founded, only frankly, I have felt that it is not quite as difficult as many others. The "Pit" is so named because a hole was simply dug in the ground and floor laid in the bottom of the hole, seats put on all four sides, and a roof put overhead. There is only one entrance/exit from the floor, a long steep tunnel at one corner of the arena. Seating capacity is approximately 18,000, and it is usually filled for every game.

The first experience I had in the "Pit" was when I was an assistant at the U of O. It was in its second year of existence, and the UNM team was undefeated in it at the time. After a very hard fought game, we won 61-59. During our hasty exit up the tunnel, our players and coaches were sworn at, spit on, and had coke thrown at us. Hard loosers, those folks. While we were in the showers, the scorekeeper entered our dressing room and informed Coach Belko that he had recounted the score, and that we only had won by one point, 60-59. Belko shouted to the players, "Hurry up and get dressed, and let's get out of here before we lose this game."

The University of Texas at El Paso is another place that has established quite a reputation. Don Haskins' team were particularly tought to beat at their old cracker box. In 1976, however, they opened a new spacious arena with 12,000 chair seats. The first year of its existence, poor Don's team didn't win a single conference game at home. Rumor was that Don was going to set fire to it, thus forcing his games to be played in the old place.

My first year at BYU was played in UTEP's old gym. At halftime we took the floor to warm up. The five starters were on the floor and the subs were sitting on the bench waiting for the tip off. As I was about to sit down, I saw an elderly man; probably in his early 60's who had obviously been tipping a few during the half-time break (and probably a few beforehand) walk behind our bench, whack one of our players on top of the head with the palm of his hand, and blurt "you trash." I just stood there, half shocked, half laughing as he staggered past me and took his seat in the bleachers.

The new pavilion is constructed in a such a way that the fans can't walk behind the bench, so we don't need helmets. But we could sure use ear-plugs on occasion. The floor is elevated so that the teams are sitting in a pit adjacent to the floor. Behind the players' seats is a row of benches for the radio announcers, press, statisticians, etc. The first row of fans starts just behind this row. Our radio announcer, Paul James of

KSL in Salt Lake City sits directly behind me and directly behind him is a UTEP season ticket holder that has got to be one of the most foul-mouthed, obscene, and abusive fans in the history of the sport. As I undertand it, he is an owner or part owner of a major slack manufacturing firm. Each game he sits with his lovely wife, who simply must die in anguish at his immaturity while he makes such a fool of himself during a game.

One year we were involved in a two-pointer with UTEP, and this guy seemed to be going out of his way to lean over Paul James' shoulder to shout obscenities into his microphone for the listening audience to hear. Finally, in disgust, Paul stood up, turned around to confront this guy, and said over the mike, "Here folks, let's listen to what a real UTEP fan has to say," and thrust the microphone in front of this jerk's face. For the first time in years, he had nothing to say. He simply sat down, ears twitching in either embarrassment or anger, as his wife poked him in the ribs with her elbow.

The University of Wyoming is building a new multi-million dollar basketball and athletic complex. It's going to be a welcome sight for the opponents who have played for years in the Old Cowboy Fieldhouse. The students are placed right behind the visitors' bench. After the long hard winters in Laramie, it is understandable that they release their tensions at the weekend basketball games. And they have a lot of tensions to release.

One night prior to tip off, the Wyoming coach, Jim Brandenburg (who is a great guy, and for whom I have a lot of respect) and I were visiting. Our conversation led us to a discussion of the crowds at various universities. He complained to me about an incident that he was involved in two weeks earlier at UTEP. He explained how he was hit in the back of the neck with a penny someone had thrown from the stands. We both agreed that our conference administrations must take strong stands for positive crowd behavior, or we could, in time, have a real problem on our hands.

The game started, and as usual we found ourselves involved in another donney brook with the Cowboys. The place, although it was not packed, was jumping. About 10 minutes into the game there was a call made that seemed to meet with displeasure from both benches. The poor ref couldn't satisfy anyone, since he was blasted by both coaches. About then, "WHACK," something hit me behind the ear and fell to the floor in front of me. A penny! Half smiling as I remembered my conversation with Jim, I picked it up and put it in my pocket. About then "WHACK" this time right on the top of the head. Another penny! Time out! As the players walked towards their respective benches I walked up to Jim, took his hand in mine, slapped the two pennies into his, closed his fingers over them so they were held firmly in his fist, and said, "Here Jim, I didn't get them at UTEP!" and walked back to my bench. To Jim's credit he went directly to the announcer's table, took the microphone and expressed his displeasure with the fans' throwing objects and asked that it discontinue. It did— until the next year.....

This time in our pre-game conversation, Jim and I were having a good laugh over the penny incident the year before. The horn sounded, and the players approached the benches for the announcement of the starting lineups. "And now the starting lineup for Brigham Young University." Thank goodness they weren't stones, or we would have all been dead. About 500 students stood up in unison and simultaneously threw wadded-up newspapers at our entire team as we were huddled together. It looked, for a moment, like it was raining manna from heaven. Jim got them to stop throwing pennies that sting, now we've got to work on the other things.

Thrown objects do concern me seriously, however. I have been fortunate during my coaching career to not have been involved with any really ugly situations. I have, however, been witness to a couple near misses that could have been tragic. Once, after having lost to a fine Utah State team at Logan, Utah, an irate fan threw a plastic object and hit one of our players in the eye. He went to the floor like he was shot. Fortunately he was shocked and frightened more than he was hurt, but it could have been very serious.

The first year I coached at BYU we beat the University of Utah at Salt Lake City 84-83. On our way to the dressing room I was hit with an empty can. Of far greater concern, however, seconds later one of the Ute cheerleaders ran up to our center Troy Jones and punched him in the face. It was a "hit and run" accident. Troy stands 6 foot 9 inches and the cheerleader only stood 5 feet 9 inches. The University of Utah officials dismissed him from his cheerleading position.

The BYU fan has, for the most part, been a courteous, non-hostile supportive group. They have always appreciated quality play and have never hesitated to show their appreciation to either our own players or to opponents. Their expressions of approval of our play are too numerous to mention. One well worth mentioning, however, occurred in a game in December of 1979, BYU vs. LaSalle. It was to be one of the great college games ever, as far as excitement and fan appeal was concerned. The game was for the championship of the 1979 Cougar Classic. LaSalle had the All-American Michael Brooks, who was eventually to be voted the NCAA College Player of the Year. The game was a classic. BYU pulled ahead by 10, then LaSalle tied it and went ahead by 10. Then the lead changed hands or was tied numerous times. At one stretch in the second half, Michael Brooks scored 28 consecutive points for his team. No other LaSalle player scored during that stretch. The game went into a triple overtime with BYU finally winning 108-106. Brooks ended up with a game high of 51 points, having scored in every way possible. It was the single best performance I had ever seen by one man in a college basketball game, and I have seen some great ones. (Bill Walton's 21 for 22 field goals against Memphis State in the 1973 NCAA finals is certainly a very close second.)

During the award cermonies as the all-tourney team was being announced, prior to the naming of the tournament MVP, the crowd began to chant MICHAEL—MICHAEL—MICHAEL in anticipation. He was then announced as the recipient of the award, and 23,000 fans stood on their feet and gave a deafening roar of approval of appreciation for and in honor of a great young man and a great basketball player. I'm sure that tribute from the opposition crowd was a moment that Michael Brooks will never forget.

MICHAEL—MICHAEL—MICHAEL

Someone once said that beauty is in the eyes of the beholder. The home crowd—it's a beautiful sight. The crowd when you play away from home—now that's another story.

As competitive as the world of basketball is, it has always pleased me to note that for the most part coaches and players are usually quite close and very good friends off the court. They seem, as a whole, to deal with the pressures and emotions of a heated contest far greater than certain fans. Coaches and players normally deal with difficult situations with controlled restraint. I believe that most fans do as well; some, however, are absolute basket cases. The majority live and die with their teams in the moments of glory or despair. Who was it that once said, fans are like a fickle wife—there are times when it's hard to live with them, but it is sure a lot better than trying to live without 'em.

BYU's Number One Fan — President Dallin H. Oakes.

11

WHAT'S IT ALL ABOUT?

What's it all about, this game called basketball? I guess the answer to that question would depend on one's association with the game. Basketball is many different things to different people.

To the fan, I suspect basketball is a social occasion. For the student fan, perhaps, it's waiting in line all day to get good seats. It's the excitement of going to the game with a new date, or just going to the game with a bunch of friends to get involved.

To the adult fan, basketball is getting season's tickets and hoping for the best possible seats. It's meeting good friends before, during, and after the game. Hopefully, it's also meeting some of the players personally and the joy of seeing children get their autographs.

For all fans, basketball is the sheer excitement and the pageantry of game night. It's living and dying with the team's successes and failures. It's offering the players and Coach constant advice, although no one hears it except those few people within earshot. It's giving the referee a piece of one's mind, or directing a verbal blast to the opponent's star or coach—or maybe just the guy in front who always seems to stand up and block the view of the court.

For the parents, basketball is witnessing every emotion known to man. It's sharing their son's joy in the accomplishment of successfully making the team, or his sorrow if he does not make the final cut. It's the feelings of pride when he does something particularly well during the course of the game, the heartache that surely comes when he has the misfortune of making a critical mistake, or the embarrassment when he does something foolish.

Basketball is the peace of mind that parents feel when their son is playing satisfactorily, or the frustration that they have when he is not seeing enough action. It is the sense of happiness of seeing him make a basket or get a rebound, or make an assist. It is the tendency to get angry and blame his teammate or his coach if he is not playing well. It is the fear of his being hurt seriously when he takes a hard fall, and the feeling of relief when he gets back up.

Basketball is keeping track of his points at the game, taking pictures of him and his teammates, keeping a scrapbook of his accomplishments.

Basketball is buying him a new pair of sneakers, new sox, new shorts, new t-shirt. It is washing his new sox, his new shorts, his new t-shirt.

Basketball is driving him to his games when he is young, and watching him play. It is practicing with him, coaching him.

Basketball is buying him another pair of new sneakers, washing his old sox, his old shorts, his old t-shirt.

Basketball is time—and suddenly it's all over.

The person who benefits the most from this great game of basketball is the player. For him it offers a great deal more than for anyone else.

In the beginning, it's just another way of having fun with his buddies. That concept should never be lost. But eventually a great deal more than fun and games materializes. He begins to understand the need for and the value of many hours of long, hard work, if success is the ultimate goal.

Basketball continues to be fun, but it takes on additional meaning. He now begins to know the feeling of physical pain and exhaustion as he embarks on his pre-season training programs. Basketball is now soreness, stiffness, aches and pains. In time it passes and is replaced by supreme physical conditioning. Basketball is now strength and vigor. It is self-satisfaction in knowing that the body has become a well-oiled, finely-tuned machine that is capable of accomplishing great, physical feats of strength and stamina.

But there is much more in store for the basketball player. The world of competitive athletics is one of the great ways a young man or woman can become a well-rounded individual. It affords not only physical growth, but emotional, social, mental and spiritual growth as well.

I know of no activity that parallels competitive athletics in providing young men and women opportunities for emotional growth. In every practice, and in every game, the player is confronted with moments of stress in which he has a unique opportunity to work with his emotions. Examples such as being "shut out" by his defender; committing costly turnovers; not being able to stop his man from scoring; having his coach, his teammates, the fans express displeasure with his performance: all are situations that could cause a player to lose control of his emotions. The most common example of all, a poor call by a referee, affects all of us: players, coaches, and fans alike. With proper guidance and counseling, a player will, in time, learn to control his emotions and handle these situations in a stable, mature manner.

I have mentioned that a basketball game is a social event. Practices and games are social events for players as well, if for no other reason than that during their daily association with teammates they learn many of the social graces of man.

They first of all have to learn how to get along with their fellow man. Teamwork is one of the single most important ingredients in the recipe for success. Without it, a team's ultimate potential will never be realized. I speak of togetherness not only on the floor, but off the floor as well. The carry-over value that these young players learn from their bond of unity is of everlasting value in their daily lives.

Leadership is a social skill that is learned well by many on the basketball floor. It amazes me how many athletes hold student body offices in their respective schools. On another plane, it's interesting to note how many former coaches go on to administration once they leave coaching.

Sacrifice—giving of one's self—is a social skill that more people in our world today need to practice. Unfortunately, not all basketball players learn this skill, but I have a firm belief that most do. Those that do not are usually the malcontents who bounce from team to team, or who cause disharmony and unrest on the team with which they are affiliated. Those that do, not only lead their team to its fullest potential, but their contributions are great in the community in which they live.

When I indicate that competitive athletics and the game of basketball can enhance one's mental growth, I do not mean to imply that it will necessarily make one a better historian, mathematician, etc. Studies, however, have indicated that physically active people are usually better organized and more alert mentally. I speak primarily of basketball contributing to a person's mental growth through strong mental health.

Two things particularly come to mind. First, a young player can fully realize his SELF-WORTH. I have seen basketball work wonders for shy, bashful, introverted young boys. I have witnessed their realization that they are unique individuals and very worthwhile human beings. Every year I look with pride at these young men as they grow and mature in their self-esteem and their capabilities. I see this growth take place as a direct result of their participation in basketball.

Second, each year I marvel when I observe a young man reach a point in his life that is difficult to come by. Many adults I know still have not realized it. That is, the ability to make an HONEST EVALUATION of one's self. Too many people today are afraid to admit that they are capable of making mistakes. Therefore, they go through life with an unrealistic appraisal of their own ability and capability. A lot of people are afraid to fail, and they never try. I have coached a few players who passionately wanted the ball for the first 37 minutes of the game. But when the game was in balance and we needed a basket to put us ahead during the last three minutes of the game, these same players all of a sudden became great "team" players and wanted to pass to someone else to let them try for the crucial basket. The great competitors want the ball, they want the chance to take the last shot because they not only have confidence in themselves, but they are not afraid to fail.

Paul Dunn, a General Authority for the LDS Church, once made a statement that we use often in our BYU dressing room. It goes something like this: "Failure is not falling down, failure is not picking yourself up one more time than you fall." Life consists of many "mini-failures." When a person is ready to admit that, he too will be able to pick himself up again and again until success will ultimately be his reward.

One more word along these lines. Each year that I have coached it seems as if I have encountered at least one player we call a "BUT HE". A "BUT HE" is a player that has yet to realize an honest evaluation of his abilities. He feels that he can do no wrong. Each time a coach addresses him to point out the fact that he made a mistake, his initial response to the coach will be, "But he..." with which he will point an accusing finger at someone else on the team. As the weeks and months of practice and counseling go by, most of these same "BUT HE's" realize the fact that they are capable of making mistakes and oftain that honest evaluation of themselves that is so essential to their mental health. Others never do.

Spiritual growth. How can basketball help a young player to grow spiritually? At Brigham Young University we strive to have our young men realize that they are children of God, each with a great deal of worth and potential. Furthermore, we want them to recognize that the Lord God has had His hand in all things and that without His divine guidance, none of us would reach our full potential. We hope that each player on our squad will worship God in his own way, according to his own religious beliefs, and that he will thank Him daily for his many blessings.

The fan, the parent, the players: Basketball has a special significance for each. Different yet similar. How about the coach? What's the game of basketball all about for a coach? Again, the answers are as varied as the coaches themselves.

Over the years coaches develop their own personal philosophy of the game. Mine has been nurtured from well over two decades of experience at all levels. I have paid my dues as a student, a player, a high school coach, a junior college coach, and ten years of working in the trenches as a major college assistant coach.

Now that I am a head coach at a major university, my philosophy encompasses that sphere of the game. It is a simple one, yet it touches all bases.

Basketball is not the most important thing in the world to me nor should it be for my players. When we recruit young men to play for us at BYU, we refer to them as prospective student-athletes, with a strong emphasis on student. They are obviously outstanding basketball players, because that is the business we are in. But we require much more than just basketball ability. We look for these things in a young prospect:

First, he must be an outstanding basketball player: One that has the potential to help keep our team ranked as one of the top twenty teams in America consistently. We look upon the top twenty as a minimum requirement. Our ambitions and goals are much more lofty.

Second, he must be a young man of outstanding character: One who can represent himself, his family, our great university, and the LDS Church with honor and dignity. It matters not what his race or religion are. We expect those young men who play for us to honor and respect the standards of the LDS Church, just as we intend to honor and respect their beliefs.

Third, he must be very serious about receiving a quality education. As important as basketball is to all of us, the first and foremost reason for a young man to attend college is to receive an education. Education, therefore, must be his top priority.

When we extend an invitation to a young man to become a student-athlete at BYU, we feel we are paying him our supreme compliment. We consider him to be one of the finest young men in the land, one of extremely high character.

Once a prospect accepts that invitation and enrolls as a student-athlete at BYU, we hope to have his exhibit certain qualities. As is always the case with athletes of prominence, either locally or nationally, a large percentage of the population look to them for example. Our basketball players are well-known young men in our community. We live in a glass house, and we are pleased with what the public sees.

We want our players to be PROUD that they are members of the BYU basketball squad. It is a privilege, not a right, and only a select few are chosen.

We hope our players will be GRATEFUL for the opportunity they have to play for us, and to receive an education at such an outstanding institution.

We further hope that our players will always remain HUMBLE and not expect special favors simply because they are blessed with athletic skills.

Finally, we expect our players to conduct themselves as CHAMPIONS. We believe that a person is what he expects to be. We believe in our program, we believe in ourselves. Several years ago I listened to a tape of Earl Nightingale's in which he stated that only five percent of the population of the world today will be successful. I do not know if his statistics are accurate, but I do know that the power of positive thinking has consistently had a profound affect on successful people. We have a saying on our basketball team, "You Gotta Believe." And we do!

My philosophy of basketball can be summarized by listing the three things we expect our players to do in every practice and in every game.

First: to play with INTENSITY
Second: to play with INTELLIGENCE
Third: to play with TOGETHERNESS

We feel that if our players can consistently play hard, play smart, and play as a team, we will be successful. What is success? Coach Wooden has a very eloquent definition of success. Mine is much simpler. "Do the best you can with what you've got."

What's it all about, this game we call basketball? It's all the things I've talked about in this chapter, and much, much more. It is my life, and yet it is not the most important thing in my life. In terms of time spent, there is no question that I have spent by far the greatest percentage of my time with my involvement in basketball.

My priorities of importance are quite different, however. The most important thing in my life is my loving wife, Bee, and the five children that I cherish so dearly, Kelly, Kris, Kipp, Gib, and Kali.

The second most important thing in my life is my church and the testimony I have of the Gospel.

The third most important thing in my life is this crazy game of basketball.

That's quite a love triangle!